SUICIDE

How To Cope When Someone You Love
Has Taken Their Own Life

WILLIAM J. HENRY

ISBN 978-1-63525-056-5 (Paperback)
ISBN 978-1-63525-057-2 (Digital)

Christian Faith Publishing, Inc.
296 Chestnut Street
Meadville, PA 16335
www.christianfaithpublishing.com

Printed in the United States of America

CONTENTS

FOREWORD

There are words we frequently hear but do not seriously consider until we are affected in some personal way.

As a survivor of the tragedy of the death by suicide of a loved one, you are now very well acquainted with such words as "guilt, confusion, despair, misery, heartache, sadness, gloom," and many others you may have never experienced before, at least not to the degree you now are experiencing them.

You are not alone although you do feel that no one else understands what you are going through. Like you and many others, I too experienced the loss of someone very dear to me by way of suicide.

It was unwanted, of course, unexpected, and even as of today leaves a void that I am sure will never be filled.

With suicide, there is never a total cessation of hurting.

No cliché such as "putting it behind you and moving on" is effective; on the contrary, the pain and memories are always with you.

But there is hope, there is help. What I and many others have learned on this journey of pain is that there finally comes a day when you can look at this tragedy in a way that is not only helpful to you but in a way that you can be a help and blessing to others experiencing this horrible time of grief.

With God's help and your own personal desire and great need to move forward, there will be a brighter day for you.

Let us begin the journey.

ACKNOWLEDGMENTS

I sincerely want to acknowledge the most helpful part the following people have played in the writing of this book:

First and foremost, I wish to thank my dear wife with whom I have shared our greatest joys and deepest pain. Through the death of our son, she has remained faithful to God and a wonderful companion to me.

Our remaining children, Beth, Becky, and Jonathan have been a source of strength and encouragement. They loved their brother very much and miss him immensely as of course his mother and I do; but they continue on this journey called life with consistent faith in God and a desire to make their lives matter in helping others.

My close friend and former Pastor, Robert P. May, Sr. has been so encouraging in his comments about the need for such a book as this and in my ability to write it. I am not an author by vocation so his encouragement has given me the confidence to attempt such an awesome task.

I wish to acknowledge Myla and Doug Kreinik for the courageous manner in which they took the tragic death by suicide of their beloved son and have turned it into a mission by which they are helping many other survivors.

Primarily, I Wish To Acknowledge The Wonderful And Faithful God We Try To Serve. He Promised To Go With Us Even Through The Darkest Times Of Life And He Certainly Has Proved That He Does Just That. He Is Worthy Of Our Trust And Praise. I Have Found That Joy And Grief Can Go Arm-In-Arm Because God Gives Us The Strength We Need To Keep Going When We Want To Quit. If Any Real Benefit Comes From The Publication Of This Book, I Give All Credit To God. Without Him, I Would Not Have The Initiative, Ability, Or Desire To Begin And Complete Such An Endeavor.

DEDICATION

This book is dedicated to all my fellow survivors who are on this difficult journey none of us chose to make.

If this book is a help and encouragement to you, its purpose will have been fulfilled.

To
The Memory of Our Beloved Joseph

DISCLAIMER STATEMENT

I feel it wise and necessary to state that I am neither an expert on mental disorders nor do I pretend to know all about the complexities of all that is involved with suicide, bipolar disorders, depression, and schizophrenia This book is written from the standpoint of a survivor, not a specialist. If you or someone about whom you are concerned feel a need to pursue definite mental health treatment, please seek professional help for proper diagnosis, evaluation, and treatment.

A LETTER FROM A FRIEND

It wasn't supposed to be this way. It was so unwanted and so unexpected—yet, one of the people you love the most has taken themselves out of your life. No longer will you see their smile, hear their voice, have sweet conversations with them, or simply enjoy the knowledge that they are there whenever you want to call them on the telephone or spend time with them. It is over. They are gone. And you are left behind.

And with their going, also gone are all the opportunities you may have had to make your relationship with them sweeter, more meaningful, and enjoyable.

Why did they do this horrible thing? Did they not realize in taking their own life, they took part of your life too?

You are a walking dead person, devoid of feelings except for a constant feeling of sadness and regret. And you do not believe it will get better. Tomorrow will be a repeat of today, and today is not a day of joy.

Why didn't your loved one talk with you before doing this? You could have talked about the problems of life and maybe could have come to a solution or at least a plan of action that might have lead to solving some of their problems. But they did not share their innermost pains and thought they could "work it out" on their own. Oh, how you wish you could go back in time—how you would plead and pray and research possible solutions and whatever else you could think to do that you believe would have helped.

But it is over. There is no going back. And the future will now be filled with memories that bring tears, regrets for what you might have done and didn't—guilt and a myriad of almost indescribable emotions.

Does it have to be this way? Is there no joy in your future? How and where can you get help with these feelings of despair and gloom?

There is an answer, and I sincerely pray that the information and message of this book will be a great help to you.

I am not an author by vocation. I am only a fellow traveler who, like you, has experienced the suicidal death of a loved one. This book is my letter to you, as one friend to another, as one who has experienced the same pain you are now experiencing.

As a parent whose beloved adult son took his own life, I know firsthand what you are now going through. I understand full-well the thoughts that daily course through your troubled mind. And although a degree of sadness will always be with you, you can still be a victorious and happy person.

There is help and there is hope. I can wholeheartedly and sincerely assure you that if you will allow God to direct your healing process and apply what he has for your life, you will again be a strong, happy and useful person. It is a process, a transition, not an overnight change. But it will come. Be encouraged and realize that as dreary as life may seem now, it can be one of joy and purpose again. With God's help, as you look to him for strength and guidance and, as you learn about the process you are going through—you will smile again.

Sincerely, with love, A Friend

Sometimes letting go takes more
strength than holding on.

—Unknown

CHAPTER ONE

You Are Lonely, But Not Alone

What a terrible sense of loneliness has gripped your heart. Sadness is a constant companion every day now.

But you are not alone. Every year in the United States alone, over 41,000 people die by suicide. Many of our precious young people, many brave veterans returning from active duty, others we never even considered would do such a thing.

Think of the many "survivors" left behind to mourn the loss and cope with all that is involved.

Fathers, mothers, brothers, sisters, other relatives, friends, coworkers, neighbors who care—all left behind to try to answer the many questions that remain: "Could I have done something to have kept this from happening?" "Why didn't I see it coming?" "Why, Why, Why?"

There are not just thousands of people trying to get through this time and doubt, there are millions of survivors just like you who are trying to cope with this heartbreak.

What are you experiencing just now?

There is no common time frame for healing and we all have our own stumbling ways of moving forward, but there are some very common reactions that nearly every suicide survivor experiences: (And we will revisit some of these and others later)

1. SHOCK: A violent, unexpected collision of emotions. Shock like you never experienced before in your life.

Unbelievable numbness and you are disoriented, as if reality has been replaced by a "foggy," unreal world where you hear and see people without really seeing them or hearing them. You can't concentrate and yet you talk with others without really understanding what is being discussed. You are experiencing the very common reaction called shock. It will pass.

2.   DEPRESSION: A hollow feeling of discouragement, a dark valley of gloom. For many people, sleep does not come easy now and there may be a loss of appetite while others eat more than normal as a therapeutic activity. You have no energy now and there is the ever-present feeling of sadness. You stare at a wall without thinking and you just want to be left alone—you are suffering depression. You will get relief from this in time—be patient with yourself.

3.   BITTERNESS OR ANGER: You may be irritated at best, furious at worst, toward the person who died and left you with this grief, toward a family member or acquaintance, a mental health worker, or even yourself. This bitter feeling of near hatred overwhelms your being to the point where you feel as if you need to act upon the feeling to "get back" at them some way for the pain they have caused you. This is normal—you are normal if you feel this. It will pass.

4.   GUILT: You continually have the thought that if only you had "done something," you could have kept this from happening. You think of different scenarios of things you wished you had done to help avoid the tragedy, thinking, "If only I had done this... " This is normal in the coping process. This seems to take longer to diminish with most people because we have such a personal attachment to the person. It will pass. Be patient and hopeful.

There are other emotions which you may experience since we have different ways of coping and different degrees of strength, but nearly every person going through this process experiences some degree of these four reactions.

"God loves us in good times and bad…
But He is even more real in our lives
when we are having tough times."

—Joe Gibbs
Former Head Coach of the
Washington Redskins

CHAPTER TWO

Closure

We have all seen reports of a child or other loved one who was murdered or otherwise harmed and the body has not been located and/or the perpetrator has not been punished. The family wants "closure." To finally have crucial questions answered and be able to "get on with their life." "Let's just tidy everything up and get back to normal living."

THERE IS NO SUCH THING AS CLOSURE

There is no "closure" as such, but that does not mean there is not relief. To expect what some people believe to be total "closure" as described by many is not only unrealistic, but can actually be counterproductive to the grieving process. Things will never be "normal" again.

Every person has their own personal bereavement process and "closure" really is only a myth. In reality, what most people call "closure" is really only justice served or vengeance realized toward the perpetrator of a crime or having no vengeance but having questions answered about what occurred with their loved one. There is a sense of satisfaction that all that could be done to bring about justice and a completion of knowing all that occurred regarding the tragedy has been ascertained.

There is not a secession of sadness and grief, only a secession of not knowing what happened.

To expect a complete loss of grief is an illusion that will not happen whether it concerns a suicide or other tragedy.

What must occur is a realistic acceptance of the facts and the need to personally deal with them. Those who are survivors of a suicide have neither satisfaction of knowing all that led up to the tragedy nor do they have any sense of justice or reason. Questions remain, along with the pain.

The pain of loss is now a part of your life and will be until you die. You will probably continue to think about the dear loved one every day and for some, many times every day.

Some remember the loved one with great sadness and intensity, some remember them with less intensity but still with great love.

They come to your mind when it is near their birthday, during holidays, sometimes just remembering where they sat at home, a certain aroma, another person looking or sounding similar to your loved one, a song, a particular restaurant or other place where you shared time with them. Looking at their picture brings tears that just won't stop—you miss them so very much. You read the obituary column in the newspaper or online and you wonder if that person did the same thing as your dearly beloved did. Your heart stays broken and you wish time could be turned back and that this really did not happen. You feel so all alone.

It did happen and you must go on.

To expect the common idea of closure—that everything can be all right again and the survivor can go back to a carefree life regarding the loved one is emotionally dangerous because it gives a false expectation. It only heightens the loneliness because the person seeking closure never gets the emotional release they expected. They feel they must have done something wrong, otherwise these emotional reactions would have ended at some point.

No matter how much time elapses since the suicide occurred, memories always remain. Do not deny them or try to push them from your mind. To try to forget them because of the pain of remembering is to deny precious times of love, of joy, of all that makes life worth living.

Grieving is hard, but necessary. True closure is not forgetting what happened as though some magic wand was waved and the problem is over. True closure is when we accept what happened and deal with the process of grieving in a mature and patient manner while remembering how much we still love the person who left us.

Perhaps God has a plan for your life that can only be accomplished by what you have gone through. All things are not good, but all things work together for good to those who love God (Romans 8:28).

Death is a part of life.

We don't like it under normal circumstances, but especially when it happens because a loved one ended their own life. Yes, it may cause shock, sorrow, and intense grief, but this is not an unusual occurrence for Christians or non-Christians. In John 16:33, Jesus plainly states this: "In the world ye shall have tribulation; but be of good cheer; I have overcome the world."

And faithful David said, "It was good for me that I was afflicted."

But "be of good cheer?" How is that possible when we have lost someone so dear to us? Yes, grief counselors help; they tell us: "Take your time, don't make any big decisions for a year, remember the good times, etc." These are helpful, but the counsel of God is ultimately the only thing that makes real sense of everything when your world has fallen apart. People ask, "How are you doing" and you don't want to answer because you are so sad that you really do not want to talk about it. But you will in time if not already.

We should not seek what many term as closure. What we should seek is God's strength and guidance that we might have his strength in our life and his guidance about how we might use this tragedy for his glory. More about this later.

Kites rise highest against the wind, not with it.

—Winston Churchill

CHAPTER THREE

Why—Why—Why???
Why Did My Loved One
Commit Suicide???

We Want To Know "Why?" Our Loved One Took Their Life. Why did they leave us so abruptly with no warning?

We go over and over the last few meetings and conversations we had with them and try to understand the reason for this desperate act.

But we determine nothing definite even though many times there are obvious actions leading up to the suicide.

In the tragic loss of my son, the reason was the same as 90 percent of all suicides in the United States: a psychiatric disorder. In most (not all) of these diagnosed psychiatric disorders, the cause of suicide is either depression, schizophrenia, or bipolar disorder. Ninety percent of all suicides are people who had a definite and diagnosable psychiatric disorder at the time of their death. Another factor can be substance abuse, either separate from the disorder or in combination with it.

These mental disorders can cause tortuous mental anguish and suffering. Any of them can cause a distinct inability to think clearly and make wise decisions. Too often, these individuals fail to take prescribed medications as they should, do not seek help, and feel they can handle the problems without outside assistance.

The combination of life's events, and challenges coupled with the constant feeling of hopelessness and the psychological pain are simply too much for the person to endure and, thus, they feel that death would be better than the agony of living.

At the risk of your thinking I am exaggerating, I need to state that my adult son (twenty-nine years old at the time of his death) was a sweet, intelligent, caring, artistic, creative, and loyal son.

Under normal circumstances, he would never bring shame or grief to our family. But being bipolar and with severe depression, life was beyond his control.

We went the usual route of counselors, one psychiatrist, treatment centers, mental health facilities, all to no eventual avail.

This seeking for help was so frustrating. We sought help, but there were seemingly no solutions. Our son felt the only solutions were either to take prescription medicines which he felt would make him become a sort of "zombie" and quench his creative abilities, or try to handle the disorder on his own terms.

Like many others with the same disorder, alcohol abuse, and drug use entered in.

But the primary danger came from the depression and pain that could only be alleviated by the drug or alcohol use.

Even though his mother and I did all we possibly could to help, and were not enablers but truly sought every avenue of help we were aware of, he took his life. We tried to remain hopeful, yet felt so helpless, right up to the end. We, like many, many others, had to come to the conclusion that just as people die from heart disease or cancer, they also die from having mental illnesses.

There is no stigma, blame, or shame to bear with this; it is just a fact that mental disorder is a cause of death as much as any other cause.

Suicide is the result of an underlying illness coupled with a confusing mix of individual circumstances.

As I have and will continue to state, suicide is not a weakness in morals or character. It is not a sign of irresponsibility nor is it an attempt to "get back" at someone. It is the tragic result of an illness, not a reason for any shame or guilt. Let this fact permeate your thinking until you accept it as fact.

Perhaps you, too, are just now starting your journey of healing.

Suicide is so complicated. We seek answers that never come. We seek relief that evades us.

Your loved one may have had what most victims experience when suffering with these illnesses: painful mental and emotional suffering—living is so difficult for them because their mind does not work as a normal person's mind works.

They suffer frequent and horrible depression. Their life is one of being almost always tired and yet they strive to achieve but only have a "window" of energy or interest each day.

There is a desperate hopelessness, where most things really do not matter to them. There are frequent changes in their mood although they try to not show it.

They like to be alone most of the time and do not want to be challenged about their behavior or inability to function normally.

They do not take pleasure in many things.

In short, except for a possible avenue of creativity or friends, life holds no joy for them. Living is a daily struggle. No one thinks as they do, no one can enter into their confused, troubled mind. No one knows the pain involved just to try to appear normal.

Often the families of these who die by suicide are close-knit and loving and do all they can to help them know they are accepted, loved, and understood. But it is not enough.

What is the mindset of the person considering suicide?

They eventually got into such a state of mind that leaving was better than staying. Sometimes, they are in a drug or alcohol-induced state and do not even realize what they are doing and sometimes the mental pain is so horrible they can stand it no more. At these times, their ability to think of the pain they leave behind as their loved ones try to cope with their decision is just not there. They would not hurt anyone under normal circumstances and with normal thinking.

But they are unable to think rationally at the time of death and have no idea how much grief they are about to bestow on the survivors. We have to forgive them.

I had ill feelings only briefly after the death of my son and only toward one person.

This person stated to me that suicide "was the most selfish thing a person could do" because of the pain it gave the survivors. Knowing my son and how much he loved his family and friends, I was offended by this callous statement. Later I realized that what the person really meant by the statement was not so much directed as a negative comment regarding the suicide victim, but his belief that any suicide brings so much terrible grief to others, grief like no other cause of death can bring. I understood it later but still do not like that comment. I think there is a much better way to express the thought.

Because suicide is so often poorly understood, many who are left behind feel ashamed or somehow stigmatized. This is not good nor fair nor necessary.

Mental disorders very often involve severe changes in the functioning of the brain to the point where the affected person has extreme difficulty in controlling their moods and behavior. Living is a struggle because their mind struggles continually. Only periodic attempts at happiness bring about a temporary resting of the mind.

Once someone in this condition entertains the idea of suicide and seriously considers it, even mentally plans it, there are limits as to how much friends and loved ones can do to prevent it.

There is help and there have been many victories wherein a possible suicide has been averted and the person lives a satisfying life.

However, it is tragic and heartbreaking, that oftentimes, there is so little anyone can do to stop it. There is hope and there are medications and therapy; some are helped by these avenues, some are not.

Be realistic and understand that there was only so much you could have done to prevent this from happening. As with any illness, physical or mental, we do all we can to help. But inevitably, we must accept the result of that illness, go through the process of regaining some semblance of normalcy in our lives and not let the death of our loved one be the ultimate event that keeps us from future happiness and progress.

Courage is not the absence of fear; it is being afraid
but continuing to do what needs to be done.

—Unknown

CHAPTER FOUR

What About Holidays And Birthdays?

First, keep in mind that there is no set way to celebrate annual holidays and birthdays. It will differ between people and events and how you feel is best to continue the celebrations.

Do what you find meaningful and comfortable, not what everyone else expects of you. You may find, in time, that how you now feel about celebrating the holiday will change.

For birthdays, some people simply ignore it, some celebrate with friends and family, reminiscing about the loved one and some spend the time in private recollection.

Whichever meets your needs at this time is what you should do. Of course, the feelings of others, especially close family members, need to be considered. Be sure to talk openly with them so the event does not become a source of hurt feelings or misunderstandings, but becomes another way to honor and remember the loved one.

Whichever avenue of remembering and celebrating you choose, tell your family and friends your feelings and thoughts. Talk to them. Do not wait for them to talk with you because they may not know what to say or what is expected of them. It will relieve them to know just how you are coping, what your plans are for the holiday, and how they can best be a part of it. And do not be afraid to openly speak of your loved one by name, not a vague reference, but their name. This frees others to do the same and ultimately will bring joy and comfort to each of you. It will hurt at first, but, in time, it will actually bring joy to you.

Do not let the event become a time of misery as you reflect on the past, but let it be a time of sweet memory. Certainly you and the other remaining loved ones will look upon each holiday in their own individual way. Some will want to openly discuss the memories of the past, some may even want to discuss the suicide itself as a way to help bring about a better level of coping while others may want to reverently and quietly discuss memories and time shared with the loved one. Do not feel guilty if you laugh at some of the memories of things that happened regarding your loved one. Laughter may seem disrespectful at first, but as you heal, you will find it easier to see that laughter is a normal and correct emotion in this ongoing process.

Make certain you do not allow the holiday to become a time of overly observing the place your loved one held in the family. Yes, their memory is precious to you because they were and still are precious to you. But too often, the remaining family members are neglected at holidays by too much emphasis being placed, year-after-year, on the departed loved one. Those remaining need love and attention too and should not be relegated to a lesser place in the family traditions.

Again, be patient with yourself and realize that time will bring about positive changes as you celebrate each of the holidays. For now, do what you feel most comfortable in doing. Remember, the ultimate goal is to celebrate the true purpose for the particular holiday with your remaining family while still including the loved one by way of remembering them in a proper way.

It may take a good while to find what you believe is the "correct" approach toward celebrating the different events. Again, be patient with yourself and others.

"People need love, especially when
they do not deserve it."

—Unknown

CHAPTER FIVE

What To Expect From Friends And Acquaintances

You have entered a world unlike any you ever expected or even knew existed. It is a world of questions, of memories that bring pain regardless of whether they are memories of "good times" or "bad times." You hurt and nothing seems to help, at least not permanently. In the processing of this time of grief, this is as it should be. If there were no tears and no emotional pain, it would not be natural.

A person cannot grieve without first loving. You loved the person who took their life, therefore you grieve. You are normal.

Please be aware that this is new to your friends and other acquaintances, too. They have probably never had to deal with such a tragedy either. And because of their care and concern for you, they want to help; but often they have no idea what to do or what to say.

How can you help them as they try to be a comfort to you?

First realize that the reactions of your friends and others will be as different as they themselves are different. Some will come forward and be somewhat bold in their words and actions while some will be reticent "backward" and speak quietly and with reserve and may not come around as much as they did before. Some may have sent flowers, some may have brought food, others may have given you a hug and words they felt might be of some comfort. Unless they were very exceptional, many of those tokens of care you probably do not remember due to the emotional trauma you have gone through (and possibly are still experiencing).

Remember, they are in some way going through a time of questioning and troubles, too. They may not have been as emotionally involved with your loved one as you, but they are emotionally involved with you and therefore their pain is a great pain, too, because they hurt for you and want to help.

Some people are awkward during times of crisis: they just do not know what to say or do. They want to help, but feel helpless. Be patient with them. They are hurting, too. Some people are extroverted or at least not afraid during times of crisis to express their innermost thoughts and desires to be of help. Often, these people can be irritating because it may be "too soon" for you to discuss certain things—you are just not ready to express your thoughts and feelings because you have not come to a point where you even realize exactly how you feel or what you should be thinking. Be patient with them, too. Most really want to help.

Let people know you want their help and appreciate their help. You can use this opportunity to show your concern for them, too, as they show their love for you. Too often, survivors become selfish and expect all those in their environment to focus their attention and affection on them. This is not unusual and, at first, is somewhat expected. But this should soon be replaced by everyone (including the survivors) by a general concern for all involved. Just as some people enjoy "acceptable" illnesses in order to be the center of attention, so do some suicide survivors like to remain the center of attention well after the time for this to be past is realized. This continual desire of self-centeredness is not common but does happen. For some, it is a catharsis, a way of continually dwelling on the tragedy as a means of coping with it. But no one area of our life should control all other areas of our life—there should be balance and this even includes tragic events in our life.

When and if you need help with something, ask for it. Most of your friends and acquaintances will be glad to help and even honored that you asked them. Do not feel that it is an intrusion on their lives to be asked; they welcome the opportunity. Helping you helps them.

Expect others to avoid talking about the suicide even if you bring up the subject. They are afraid they might say the wrong thing and may be misunderstood. Let them know when you are ready to talk and share deep feelings. With some people, you will never want to discuss certain things; with others, you truly want to have their thoughts and comments. Let them know this. If the friend is a close and trusted friend, talk much to them. You need to hear your own voice say what is going on inside your head and though it may be confused and emotionally draining, it is good to talk about your innermost concerns. A true friend will listen and love and not judge. It will help them help you.

Let people show their love for you. You need your "quiet times," yet you should not become a recluse. Let others be a part of your life through visits to you and your being a part of activities involving others. If you feel comfortable in doing so, call certain friends on the telephone and let your conversation "flow," talking about many areas of mutual concern and interests. It will at least start the way back to normal relationships with others.

If certain friends try to control your time, let them lovingly know that you are not ready for continual activity, but need time alone. If they love you, they will understand. A true friend will do what is best for the other friend regardless of their own feelings.

Grieving is physically and emotionally very tiring. It saps your energy. During the process of grieving, you will become tired much quicker than before. Let people know this fact and that you may have to lie down for short periods of time during the day. This has nothing to do with your sleeping habits at night. You may or may not have trouble sleeping at night, but you probably will be experiencing periods of fatigue during the day regardless of how well you may have slept the previous night. Do not deem yourself rude or anti-social if you feel it necessary to excuse yourself from an individual conversation or group activity. This is part of the process for most survivors.

Take time to write personal notes of appreciation to all who have helped you thus far. This might include those who sent flowers, food, or other material assistance. It could include a note to the funeral home, a doctor, the pastors involved, coworkers, friends, and others who helped in a material or non-material way. If what they did for you meant much to you, it will mean much to them to receive a note of appreciation from you.

When it would be appropriate, and only if you are on a level in your grieving process where you are aware of your true emotional condition as you write the notes express your true feelings of how their part in the event helped you. This will be a blessing to them and will help you with the grieving process.

In time, you will develop strength that will allow you to satisfactorily return to what was your routine manner of living.

This will include your relationships with friends and acquaintances. It will never be the same as it was, but it will be good.

For many, the relationships with several friends and acquaintances will be stronger and sweeter because it gave opportunity to "really know" those involved in your life.

The darkest clouds can have beautiful silver linings that we could not have seen without the darkness.

Be kind, for nearly everyone you
meet is fighting a hard battle.

—Unknown

CHAPTER SIX

Life Is Different Now

An old Elvis Presley song called Are You Lonesome Tonight? has included in it the phrase, "Do you gaze at your doorstep and picture me there?"

How often now do you mentally see the image of the person you still love so much and will miss always?

You look at their favorite chair and "picture them there" and the tears start again. As you are doing business outside the home or shopping, you see someone who has features so much like your loved one and your heart seems to "just drop" aching with pain as the emotional wound of missing them is broken open again.

You hurt and it seems just when you start to heal and go on with life something reminds you again that you lost someone you dearly love and will never see them again.

The world you once knew suddenly disappeared and a different world, one you do not like, is where you now live.

Be encouraged. It will get better. For now, please realize that others who have had the same experience as you are also going through the same trial. Most who went through it are now able to live each day with a new attitude of acceptance, and a will to move forward and have a different, but happy, outlook on life.

I recently read the obituary of a twenty-eight-year-old young man who had taken his life. His own loving father wrote the obituary and was so brave and honest in his tribute to the son he loved so much. The bold and honest way the obituary was written encouraged me because it stated many things that my family and I shared with this dear family. We had encountered many of the same efforts to help our son, similar disappointments and ultimate grief. It was obvious this young man was a loving person who was greatly loved in return by his friends and family. Some of the direct quotes from the obituary are:

> "Took his own life."
> "He had friends in all four corners of the globe yet suffered and hid deep depression."
> "We would usually talk for at least an hour."
> "He wanted to help people" "he spoke of the future ahead."
> "(He) loved people."
> "He loved his family and friends, even the strangers he just met."
> "Everyone has memories of his boisterous laughter, mischievous eyes, wacky humor, slanted smile, and willingness to help others through their difficulties."

Then the father encouraged those who wanted to honor his son to make a donation to their choice of a charity that works with alcoholism, chemical dependency, or suicide prevention.

What a brave, loving, realistic father to have written this remarkable tribute in such an honest and heartfelt manner!

During the writing of this book, I had the opportunity to spend a short time with this father and we had a sweet time of sharing memories and tears together. He is certainly to be commended. Though the suicide of his son was only a short time prior to our meeting, he and his wife had already passed the level of denial and anger and were using the tragedy to honor their beloved son and were encouraging readers of the obituary to help others in need.

They fully realized that their loved one's chemical and alcohol usage or dependency was a result of the mental condition (severe depression) not a result of an undisciplined, selfish life.

As with my son, it appears that the need for "something" to ease the pain of depression and mental torment was so terrible that using drugs and alcohol was not a source of fun and pleasure, but were the only things that brought about a temporary relief from the horrible mental anguish.

It is encouraging to hear stories of survivors and how they are progressing. It honors their loved one and encourages others to keep moving forward in the coping process. This is one of the great benefits of support groups.

It hurts now when someone makes flippant statements using the word "kill" as in, "I would kill for a good steak" or (worse), "I could have just killed myself I was embarrassed so much."

You continue to feel guilty and think of all the things that possibly could have been done or should have been done to prevent the suicide.

Some memories make you very sad even while there is a subconscious fear that you will not remember the loved one as much or as well as you should.

When you hear of a suicide, you automatically hurt for the family.

When you see the obituary of a young person, you wonder if it was a suicide. You may even find yourself reading the Obituary Column every day now with this thought in mind.

You find a book, article of clothing, or other item you think your loved one would like and you consider it for them, only to immediately realize they are no longer in your life. It hurts so much.

Your grief makes you cry more often and it does not take much to start the tears flowing. You are much more emotional than before.

You may find yourself more irritable than before. Things and people get on your nerves quicker than they once did.

You read or hear of troubled individuals who possibly were arrested for being in trouble with the law and you wonder if they, too, may have a mental inadequacy rather than a true problem with discipline or character.

You try to recall last conversations and you yearn for just a few minutes more of their presence, sadly realizing that it will not happen.

You catch yourself just shaking your head in disbelief and sorrow.

Physical pain sometimes goes along with the emotional pain. You may have heaviness in your chest, frequent unexpected crying, and sighing very often as you recall the loved one.
Some people are not able to sleep very well at first and, as was stated earlier, you may feel very tired during the day even if you slept well the night before.

Concentration may be a problem and you may feel as if your mind is "in a fog." Focusing on one thing is more difficult than before.

You may want to live in isolation as much as possible.

You feel that no one else understands what you are going through and the comments of others, no matter how well-intentioned, do not bring comfort. The comments may even bring more anguish and possibly anger.

When you meet or hear of someone who is experiencing the same tragedy you are experiencing, there is an immediate bond. You want to reach out to them to comfort them and hopefully receive some semblance of comfort in return. They understand.

Sympathy is a feeling of concern for others who may be going through a difficult time, but those with empathy are going through the exact experience through which you are going—they know first-hand exactly how you feel.

When you are in a conversation with another, you wonder if they are discussing one subject, but at the same time are thinking of the suicide and wondering about your mental or emotional condition.

Sometimes you feel a vague sense of being frightened, but you do not know what frightens you. It is a sense that life is not under your control as it was once.

Your emotional life now is like a roller coaster ride of emotions: some days are "pretty good" and some are not so good. Even within a day, your emotions fluctuate depending on the activities of the day and who you spend the time with. This healing process is not an orderly progression but one that can put you on many levels of acceptance or grief within a short period of time.

These are just a small few of the many emotions and thoughts others have encountered as they struggle with the pain, memories, confusion, conflicts, guilt, questions, stigma, and great loss of their loved one. You sigh and wish, "Oh, that we could only go back and that it never happened." But it did happen and you must deal with it.

You reap that which you sow. As you continue on your journey and apply what you learn, you should gradually and continually come to a point in your life at which you will again find yourself somewhat happy, functional, and enjoying a life that is again fruitful and meaningful.

Please remember these three key points:

1. There any many people going through exactly what you are enduring now. As one person put it so well, "You are now a member of a large club you never wanted to join." As stated earlier, you are lonely but not alone.
2. There is definite help and you will find that help as you continue your journey.
3. Do not create unnecessary stress for yourself by being too quick to expect relief from the grief you now are experiencing.

There is no set schedule or time frame for this type of healing. Keep patiently striving forward and you will eventually—in your own time—come to a point where life is again manageable and good. Although life may seem so bleak and sad now, it will not always be that way.

You will get better and stronger.

"Sometimes God calms the storm—and sometimes
He lets the storm rage and calms His child."

—Unknown

CHAPTER SEVEN

How Can I Endure This Pain?

They call us "survivors" but how do we survive this tragedy? What do we do?

We have never in our life had to deal with such a horrible experience. Rarely does one read books about suicide until it affects them directly and it is difficult to learn about the process while you are experiencing it. Your mind does not want to accept all you are going through.

There is help. There is a way to survive the pain. And your time frame and rate of progress may be different from any other person but will be just as effective. Though there may be times when you believe you just cannot go on with life, you can and will survive the pain.

Here are some suggestions that may help:

1. Realize that some level of guilt is normal but not necessary. It was not your fault, you are not to blame, you were not responsible. Even if there were troubling signs before the suicide, you still could not have anticipated it nor prevented it.

2. The loved one who took their own life was not rejecting you, they were rejecting the pain of living. They were not

escaping from you, they were escaping from a tortured life. They were ill, and suicide was not a statement of their feelings toward you, it was a result of their illness.

3. Use the suicide to help others. Instead of it being the negative focus of your own life, let it become an avenue of positivity as you help others who have gone through or are going this tragedy.

4. You may never fully comprehend the frame of mind of the loved one at the time they took their life. It does no good to keep asking, "Why did they do this terrible thing?" In some situations, the answer is obvious while in other situations, questions will always remain.

5. To begin to enjoy life again is not wrong nor a betrayal of your loved one. They would want you to enjoy life. To begin again to enjoy some aspects of your life is a good sign that you are healing as you should.

6. If your own physical health is not as it should be, you may need to consult with a doctor. It would be good to get a regular check-up and you can share your experience with your doctor who may offer specific help.

7. It may be painful at first, but many people find it comforting (or at least helpful) to start a journal of their thoughts, their emotions and their activities. It is cathartic (emotionally cleansing) and may help you better realize your personal rate of progress.

8. Some find it helpful to get involved in music, literary, or art endeavors. Join a musical group (choir or local singing group), start or continue art classes, write poetry or short stories or other areas of interest you may have.

9. Get involved in a support group or church setting where you have opportunity to talk with other people who truly care about you and what you are going through.

10. As stated in another place, be aware that your emotions will come in waves of different degrees of sadness. Some waves of sadness will be very unexpected and will make

you feel so alone and sad. But please remember this is normal and will diminish in time.

11. Birthdays seem to be one of the most difficult times. So often you will think, "They would have been (whatever age) this coming birthday." Or it may be a wedding anniversary, "We would have been married (number of years) this (date)." Holidays such as Christmas are difficult. What do you do? You can continue established traditions, modify them, or completely change them. It is up to you. Time will make it easier so do not feel that what you are trying to determine now will always be the way you look at upcoming times of remembering.

12. If you know of someone who is experiencing the same type of grief as you, do not compare your progress with theirs. They may heal sooner or later than you. You may experience pain they do not experience. Each survivor grieves at their own pace and own level of pain. It is an individual process not a set pace for everyone.

13. One of the loneliest times in your life will be when you visit the grave site of your loved one. You stare at the tombstone or marker, read again the name and dates and whatever else may be inscribed on it, and the tears will freely flow again. You gently shake your head back and forth in sadness, quietly cry, stay awhile, then go home. You are normal. Each person has his or her own way of grieving at the cemetery. Some people go often, some rarely can make themselves go because of the pain, and some go only on holidays; some change flowers as the seasons change. It will be as different as people are different.

14. You will probably have to encourage most others to talk about the suicide and the loved one. Very often, your friends and acquaintances are reluctant to try to discuss it with you because they do not know your emotional condition. Help them. They often do not know what to say so say nothing about it. Share your heart with them. In

doing so, it will allow them to share their love for you as they express their thoughts.

15. Do not be reluctant to ask for help whether it be physical or mental. Physically, you may need help with your household chores or repairs. Mentally, you just may need to talk with someone, ask for their advice or assistance in making decisions. Do not deprive them of the opportunity to express their love or concern to you. You may feel you are "bothering" them, but they will look at the opportunity as a time of joy to be a blessing in some way to you. It will help them to help you.

16. Find a comfortable way of telling others how your loved one died. It will vary from person to person depending on how close a relationship you have with the people you are talking with. One common statement that seems to be a good one for most survivors is this, "He or she had (whatever illness or cause, such as severe depression) and took their own life." Or you may simply want to acknowledge that your loved one died by suicide without further explanation. Do not feel ashamed to tell others about it but do not feel obligated either. Choose whichever is best for you. You are not obligated to explain to anyone what occurred and you will find that time will give you the way that is best for you to tell others how the death came about.

What do you do now? Keep on going, keep on living, keep on this journey, having faith that the journey will end in a good place and with good results.

God did not promise us smooth
sailing, but a safe harbor.

CHAPTER EIGHT

Facts About Suicide

Let us pause a short while in our journey to observe some facts about how and why people take their own lives, as well as some related facts. These may not necessarily be helpful in our personal healing process but are important things to know when thinking about our individual situation and when discussing the subject of suicide with others. We might use these facts as we discuss this subject with others.

There are so many misunderstandings about suicide. Let us see truth, not what people incorrectly suppose. Here are some questions that often come to the forefront of conversations regarding suicide:

1. Is suicide an inherited condition?
ANSWER: Most (not all) authorities would answer No.

It is true that certain suicide-related factors tend to be prevalent in families. These may be varying degrees of depression, bipolar illness, or other risk factor. This definitely does not ensure that you or another family member will become severely depressed, bipolar or die by suicide. Often, people who have had a loved one die by suicide think about doing the same thing while going through their time of grief; this is not good, but it is not unusual. Most never carry out the action and it is not due to any hereditary condition.

If there is a true awareness of severe depression or other related illness in any survivor, that individual should get a professional evaluation to determine their mental or emotional condition.

There have been studies that indicate a higher risk for suicide between identical twins, biological children of those who have taken their own life, and members of a family in which they were exposed to a suicide. However, this in no way suggests that a suicide in the family necessarily heightens the risk for all remaining family members. Awareness of the possibility for risk and paying close attention to any signs of mental or emotional problems needs to be addressed whether or not there has been a suicide in the family, but especially if it did, in fact, occur in the family.

2.   Are most deaths by suicide caused by a selfish desire to punish the survivors who may have made the life of the victim difficult?
ANSWER: A resounding No.

Generally (not always) for those who take their own lives the pain of living is greater than the pain of dying.

Studies show that very often suicide and attempts at suicide are totally unplanned and occur at times of extreme mental conflict, not when there is a conscious awareness of what is happening to them.

3.   How often are suicides committed in the United States?
ANSWER: Latest statistics show that over 41,000 suicide deaths occur per year in the U.S. Death by suicide is the tenth leading cause of death for American citizens with someone dying by suicide every 12.8 minutes.

4. What is the most common cause for suicide?
ANSWER: Some form of mental disorder or illness.

Most who die by suicide (at least 90 percent) suffered from some sort of mental illness. For some survivors, it is difficult to think of their loved one having had a mental illness, but this is exactly what it was in most situations. The most common mental illness, extreme depression, is often accompanied by intense feelings of hopelessness, desperation, a constant (or at least frequent) state of anxiety, or another intense emotional or mental disorder. They were not lacking in character or morals, they were ill. Often, as a result of these confusing and painful disorders in their life, these tormented individuals turn to illicit or prescription drugs, alcohol, or other harmful avenue they feel will help them deal with the pain of living. This, of course, places them at a higher risk for committing suicide.

5. Is suicide more prevalent in males or females?
ANSWER: Males.

Males constitute about 75 to 80 percent of all suicides and use more lethal methods such as firearms while females normally use medication or some other form of poison as a suicide method. About 75 percent of all non-fatal attempts of suicide are attempted by females. The use of firearms constitute more than half of all the methods of suicide.

6. At what time of the year do most suicides occur?
ANSWER: In the Springtime, mainly in the month of April.

Contrary to popular belief, more suicides do not occur during the Christmas season. December actually is the month with the lowest rate of suicides.

7.   If a person openly talks about suicide does that mean they really are not going to carry it to its final end?
ANSWER: It does not mean that at all.

Most (not all) people who actually die by suicide have confided in someone else that they are considering doing so. Sadly, the ones they confide in are in many cases not close family members who take their comments seriously; or possibly they did confide in a family member but the family member did not realize how serious was the mental condition of their loved one.

This should not be a point for guilt or anger. Most survivors feel regret for things they felt they should have known or done to prevent the suicide. But in reality, the great probability exists that eventually the suicide would possibly have occurred no matter how diligently the survivor tried to help.

8.   Is this statement true: "Time heals all wounds?"
ANSWER: Sadly, the answer is No.

While there may be some easing of the survivor's pain as the months and years go by, it seems your life is stuck in one long, sad day. Time will not heal you but you will progress if you face the tragedy head on and engage in an intelligent and meaningful process of recovery. It is not the passage of time that helps but what you do as the time passes. We will see in later chapters some sources of help.

9.   Does media coverage affect the number of suicides?
ANSWER: Yes, it can.

You have heard of "copycat" crimes, wherein a person emulates (copies) the method or type of crime he or she has seen portrayed over and over in the media. With communication being what it is today with television and the internet flooding our society with information overload, the suicide of a prominent person becomes a media frenzy. This can and has resulted in vulnerable and troubled individuals "copying" the same method the famous person utilized. If you are aware of a severely depressed individual who you feel might become a victim of suicide and with whom you have a close relationship, it may be wise to quickly start a dialog with them about the suicide (in a manner not alluding to their own disorder).

10. Will I be able to find some sort of peace even though this tragedy has totally changed my life?

ANSWER: Yes, assuming you keep moving forward in this long process of grief. Do not give up. In life, there are no problems too large to conquer, there are only people who remain too small to conquer their problems.

When one door closes, another opens; but we often look so long and so regretfully upon the closed door that we do not see the one which has opened for us.

—Alexander Graham Bell

CHAPTER NINE

Reflections On The Grieving Process

We touched on the process of grieving in an earlier chapter, and I do not wish to be redundant in the presentation of that which may be of help; however, since we have discussed much material since our encounter with these points, I do believe it would be a good idea to again visit some of the key elements of healing and expand on some others.

It will take weeks and maybe even months for you to be able to rationally take hold of your emotions and thoughts. And, as I also stated earlier, regardless of how much we are able to conquer our pain and emotional "ups and downs," the pain of our loss will always be with us.

Years will go by and the pain will still be with you; memories will bring pain just as when you first received the news of your loved one's death.

But these moments of hurting and pain will grow further and further apart.

Just being aware of what is happening can be a positive element in our lives and can help with the healing process.

Your world is no longer like it was. It will always be different than it was. When your loved one died, much of you died with them. But your life does not have to be a world of negative emotions and pain. You can continue living and living a life of productivity and happiness if you give yourself time and make a concerted effort to progress.

You will not only survive but you will continually become stronger and more effective in helping yourself and others.

Let us again review some of the key elements of healing as we expand on some related thoughts:

Shock was the first thing you encountered. If improperly touched, a "live" electrical wire will shock the person who touched it. This is good because the shock keeps one from more serious damage.

Emotional shock is really a good thing, too, because it provided a numbness for your mind and emotions as you initially encountered the horrible news. It gave your mind and body time to recover from the overwhelming news and should be looked upon as a blessing, not a problem.

Denial probably soon followed or possibly even accompanied the shock. Your mind refused to believe it really happened, that there was some mistake. This is normal and maybe even somewhat helpful. But eventually reality sinks in and we must admit and accept the truth.

Anger often occurs. Who caused this horrible thing? Who is to blame?

It is only natural that when you are hurt you wish to strike back at the person hurting you. There is an adage which states: "Hurting people hurt people."

Also, there is an old song entitled "You Always Hurt the One You Love" and in it is the phrase which continues the thought of the title by stating, "The one you shouldn't hurt at all."

Often, at times of extreme grief, harsh, unkind words are said which would never be uttered under normal circumstances.

SUICIDE: HOW TO COPE WHEN SOMEONE YOU LOVE
HAS TAKEN THEIR OWN LIFE

Grieving people often say hateful or hurtful words that they later greatly regret. If you have done this, ask for forgiveness from those you may have offended and do not forget to forgive yourself.

Guilt is a common response in acts of suicide. You turn inwardly to search your heart and mind to try to determine why you were not able to stop the suicide. You believe you did not do enough to prevent it.

You berate yourself for not doing everything possible and you feel that you failed. This, too, is normal and is a natural reaction to the pain you are experiencing. You are not God. You can only do so much. This feeling of guilt will pass.

Isolation possibly is a problem now. You just want to be by yourself most of the time. This is not unusual but should be temporary. Let others enter your life and help you as you share your grief with others who care about you and want desperately to be a blessing to you.

Do not deprive them by trying to be overly self-sufficient.

If this happened to someone you love, you would want to express your care for them. You will help your friends by letting them help you.

Loneliness is now your constant companion, even when you are with others, even when you are in a crowd.

You think that no one else understands the grief you now bear and they probably do not understand unless they, too, have experienced the same tragedy as you. In your loneliness, you find yourself crying quite often.

Please remember that even the strongest of people cry and it is not a sign of weakness; it is a sign that you are a loving person. The loneliness you now endure will soon not be as difficult as it is now.

Sensitivity to words of others is a problem with many people going through this time of trial. Be patient with those who make statements that may be painful when they intend to say words of comfort.

Often, people just do not know what to say and say phrases that are more hurtful than helpful. The chatter of well-meaning people is irritating to you and you just want to be away from them.

Keep in mind that most of them truly care for you and want to be a blessing; they just have not been in the extreme place of pain in which you now find yourself.

Be patient with them. Later you will be glad you were patient.

Very few things seem to matter now. This is normal and temporary.

Things that seemed so necessary and important before the suicide now hold no interest for you. You sit and stare without thinking and, when spoken to, you do not really want to engage in conversation, saying only what is expected and necessary to be polite.

Material things you felt were so valuable to you do not seem so important now.

Your appetite for food may disappear (although some during this time eat much more due to stress). Sleeping habits change. Some have great difficulty getting back to normal sleeping habits.

You feel as if you are in a dark tunnel and everyone else is at the very end of the tunnel.

Everyone else is going on with their lives and you are somehow locked into a long, lifeless existence. Again, be patient. Please know that this will get much better as you continue this process of recovery from trauma and pain. Things will matter again. Life will matter again.

Depression may be a companion you wish was not around.

Being depressed is very common in our present-day society because of the stress and pace of living we all encounter today. And admitting depression is still a stigma in some quarters although it is not a moral deficiency or lack of character.

Do not be reluctant to let others know you are having difficulty maintaining an upbeat spirit; if they love you, they will understand. With all you are going through just now, you need to talk to others about how you feel. Do not try to "tough it out" by yourself; in most cases, that is detrimental and not necessary. Feel free to cry when you feel like it. And talk to those who care about you. It is normal to become depressed during this time. It is one of the most prevalent occurrences during the healing process.

Fogginess of mind may not be a professionally-sounding term, but it certainly describes what many encounter during this traumatic time in their lives.

You may be confused and wandering mentally.

You desire to do what needs to be done, but your mind will not fully cooperate.

You try to remember names, places, dates or even people who are important to you and you have difficulty doing so; this is very typical.

You have gone through great shock and mental trauma and it will take a short while to return to what is normal for you.

You are not abnormal or permanently damaged, you are simply experiencing this confusing aspect of the healing process.

It will get better.

Selfishness or selflessness? Some people who go through what you are now experiencing become very selfish and expect the world to "revolve around them."

They become demanding and petty and often unfair in their demands of others, especially other family members.

Certainly, you need help and attention but please remember others are hurting, too, and may need comfort from you just as you need their love and care.

Then there are those who seem to always be self-sufficient and desirous of completing all tasks and responsibilities by themselves.

They simply do not want to "bother" anyone else.

A certain level of this is admirable, but during this stressful and confusing time it is wise to let others help you as you make decisions and cope with all you are experiencing.

Let others help carry your load.

They want to help and you need the assistance so it is a mutual benefit.

Everyone wants to feel needed and your friends and family not only want to help you but actually receive a great benefit from helping you.

Let them supply some of your material needs or perform needed tasks.

Lack of hope. You have never been in the confusing, depressing, and heart rendering place you now find yourself. Some people fall into the trap of thinking they will never get through this trauma and suffer needlessly for that kind of thinking.

Please believe this: you will survive and you will get through this. Be patient with yourself and with others.

Whether it is physical healing or emotional healing—it takes time for results to be seen.

"What I am is God's gift to me; what
I do with it is my gift to Him."

—Warren W. Wiersbe

CHAPTER TEN

Conversation With A Survivor

Let us go into the mind and thoughts of a suicide survivor as they discuss the route their life has taken since the suicidal death of their son.

"What were your first thoughts after it happened?"

"My first thoughts were almost unreal because I could not clearly control my mind and emotions. I was in shock and yet I knew what had happened. My mind did not want to accept that my dear son had done this horrible thing. I was horribly sad and cried almost continually. It would not sink into my mind that this was all real. I felt as though I was in a "fog" and I knew there were people around me saying many things but the words nor the people seemed to be real. What mind I possessed at the time was a mixture of extreme sadness, denial, unbelief that it happened and even some anger."

"After this, what did you do?"

"Of course, we had to be involved in the funeral arrangements and that, too, seemed unreal. It was if we were making arrangements for someone who had not actually died; I realize now it was simply part of the coping mechanism to be going from "shock" to a level of confusion and mental fogginess. But we made the arrangements and, looking back on the situation, are amazed that we were able to do this and have it turn out as well as it did. The funeral itself was a blur. It still seems like a bad dream."

"This next question may seem unkind, so if you do not want to discuss it, I am fine with that. If you feel comfortable enough to share the answer and if you know the reason, I would ask why your loved one took their own life."

"I do not mind at all discussing it. Several months have gone by now, and I can look at the death much differently that when it first happened. As with many, many others, my son had terrible depression coupled with a bipolar disorder. That was the underlying cause. The hopelessness, psychological pain, and the inability to cope with the demands of living were just too much to bear and suicide was the tragic outcome. Alcohol, drugs, and other things became a part of temporarily being released from pain. I realize now it was an illness that caused the death; it was not an act of irresponsibility or moral weakness."

"What emotions have you experienced since the suicide?"

"I have been on a mental roller coaster that seems to have no end. Some days are pretty good, some are terrible. Sometimes, I can laugh a little, sometimes I feel guilty if I laugh. Sometimes I feel so all alone even when I am with people I love. I have a tendency to want to remember all the last moments and memories of what we talked about. I miss him so much. Tears are always ready to flow and certain sights, sounds, and even smells remind me of him and make the tears start again. Things will never be the same."

"Many people suffer guilt when suicide happens in their lives. How are you doing with this?

"I felt a lot of guilt at first, and even anger at myself and other people, even anger at God. But as the time has passed and with all that I have learned about suicides, I understand now that I did pretty much all I could do. My son was sick, just like diabetes or cancer, and the disease was too much for him. I used to rebuke myself by thinking of all the things I should or could have done to prevent his taking his life. I do not think that way now. Looking back on it, I truly tried to help him in every way I could. I am limited in my experience with suicides and mental illnesses although I did try to research and learn about it. I believe very few people really understand the complexity of mental disorders and how very difficult it is to work with someone who had these problems."

"Do you have any problem telling other people that your son died by suicide?"

"At first I had trouble with this, and still do with some people I do not know very well. It was quite awhile before I came up with the exact words to say about his death. It is hard to say, 'He killed himself' or 'He committed suicide.' What I have found that helps is a simple statement, 'He had extreme depression and was bipolar and took his own life.' Then I will follow up that statement with complimentary comments about my son and what a fine young man he was. I find that most people accept this very well and it helps me to be able to have an opportunity to tell what a fine young man my son was."

"Where are you now in the healing process?"

"I think I am doing all right. I have accepted his death and I have accepted the fact that there is no place for guilt or anger. It happened and I must accept it and deal with it the rest of my life. It is extremely encouraging to talk with other survivors. No one else can help you as much as someone else who is going through the same thing. Just talking and sharing and crying together gives you so much comfort. I know this will be a lifelong journey but I hope to use it to help others and not to be a continual victim. I would encourage any survivor to read, learn, go to counseling if necessary, meet with other survivors and do not lose hope. I got better and continue to feel happier week by week as I continue my individual journey. I am at the point where I can purposely remember things my son and I did and the many great conversations we had without the memories being tormenting; it still hurts and tears still flow regularly, but the joy and appreciation for having had such a son is now greater than my grief. I see now why this is called a process; there are changes it seems, every week, for the better."

"Thank you for your courage and honesty in answering these questions."

"I do not consider myself courageous at all, just the contrary. But if my answers encourage somebody I am glad to have helped."

We cannot use something if it is broken;
God cannot use us until we are broken.

—Unknown

CHAPTER ELEVEN

What About Support Groups?

"Misery loves company."

An old, somewhat negative adage but one that has much truth in it.

It is almost astounding how there is an immediate bonding and comfort when two suicide survivors are introduced and begin to share their experiences.

It can truly be said then of each other, "I know how you feel" or "I know what you are going through." You want to hear their story and you want them to be a part of your life. There is a connection that is so very powerful one has to experience it to understand it. It is encouraging and comforting at the same time.

Many survivors find it difficult to talk openly with those who have never experienced a death by suicide. But with other survivors, there becomes almost an urgency to talk because of the mutual understanding they share. It is a great relief to talk with someone who really understands not simply sympathizes. There is such a great difference.

For a multitude of survivors, deciding to spend time with other survivors is one of the most crucial decisions they make in their healing process. It is not just "a nice thing to do," it is a vital ingredient in their progression from grief to some semblance of normalcy.

Survivors can share their grief in a safe place where others do not misunderstand the range of emotions that accompany a suicide. They listen, they care, they share their grief, too, and you understand them, too. It is a mutual support, based on a common experience and common needs.

Do not feel guilty or that you are "different" if you hesitate to attend a support group. Most survivors find it hard to start because their emotions are still so fragile. But most who do attend support groups are helped immensely as they, in turn, are a help and blessing to others. It takes no training, just honesty, listening, and a need to share.

What to expect at a support group

Not all operate the same way; possibly, in time, you too may offer suggestions that will benefit the group. But most follow a pattern somewhat like this.

Survivors sit in a circle or at least a grouping which allows everyone to face each other.

If you prefer, you may let others know that you may not want to talk during your first session. You just want to be a part of it without sharing until you feel comfortable (this usually does not take long).

Those who do speak give a brief introduction which varies per group. Some follow the pattern of letting the group know the name of the person who took their life by suicide, their relationship to the survivor, when it happened, and how it happened. The others will not be shocked because they all have similar accounts to share.

In some situations, if the new attendee feels comfortable in doing so, they are asked to speak first in the group meeting since their account has not yet been heard, and it allows them to quickly become an integral part of the group; it also allows the new member the opportunity to share something they feel very urgently needs sharing. It is a relief to be able to talk about it. There may be some general comments, then the remaining group attendees describe their present situation, experiences, and feelings.

The most positive and vital part of being in a support group is that you quickly understand that you are not alone in this frightening chain of events you are now experiencing. By listening to others, each member of the group realizes that they are truly part of a group of survivors and not alone in their pain and confusion.

Some survivors do not continue to attend group meetings, but find it comforting to frequently meet individually with members of the group. Others attend periodically, particularly at times when the grief is worse, such as birthdays, holidays, the date the tragedy occurred, or anniversaries.

Do not quickly decide not to return to a support group; it may take several visits to really feel a part of the group. Remember, you are In the midst of a process and your feelings toward many things will change as you progress.

There is a wonderful organization called the American Foundation for Suicide Prevention which has listings for over 500 suicide support groups throughout the United States. They can be reached at www. afsp.org or by calling 1-888-333-AFSP (toll-free) or 212-363-3500. (They also have a multitude of other helpful materials).

Many survivors live in areas where there is no support group; if this is so, possibly you may be instrumental in organizing a group in your area. Usually, newspapers give free notices of such meetings and, of course, there is the internet route that one could use.

If you regularly attend support group meetings, you will find that it changes from "misery loves company" to "comfort comes from company."

The road to happiness is always under construction.

—Unknown

CHAPTER TWELVE

How To Observe A Time Of Remembering

The means and methods different survivors use to remember their loved ones during holidays, birthdays, and anniversaries are as varied as the survivors themselves.

The pain of suicide is probably the greatest pain a survivor will ever encounter.

Thus, it can come rushing back into a survivor's life every time a holiday, anniversary, or birthday is near.

Some choose not to do anything special at all, simply recalling the memory of their loved one and observing their loss in a quiet and personal manner.

However, it is normally best not to spend these times alone. Whether or not a special time is planned for the event, it is best to be with others at these times.

Some choose to create elaborate and extensive presentations of affection and remembrance.

Either way, quiet or elaborate, one of the best ways to cope with them is to be aware of their nearness and plan for them. Give some thought to what you may want to do at that time that would bring comfort to yourself.

There will be a recurrence of strong emotions during these times, so you need to consider what you plan to do before the time comes.

Be prepared for times of depression and sadness on days leading up to the special time.

Take time to talk with other family members and friends if you do feel extremely sad or depressed; it will greatly help you if you do. If necessary due to extreme depression, a survivor may need to seek professional evaluation and treatment.

Be prepared to cry during this time as you again express your thoughts and emotions to others. Crying is a good release and the sign of a caring person, not a weak person.

AVENUES OF REMEMBRANCE

Again, they are so varied. Let your heart, your family, and your close friends help you as you determine which path to take to honor the memory of your loved one.

Here are just a few of the many ways survivors remember:

There are those who have established memorial funds at a mission or foundation of their choice. Usually the choice they make is one that helps other people, either with suicide-related situations or other areas of need that the survivor may feel strongly about.

Some choose to observe the memory of their one by the family getting together on the date of the tragedy (sometimes the loved one's birthday) to have a meal and time of remembrance.

There are those who travel to the gravesite and have a time of sharing thoughts, then they release helium-filled balloons with a message or picture attached.

Others place flowers at church or nursing home in honor of their loved one.

Some light candles on the anniversary of the death to commemorate that light signifies living and the loved one lives on in the survivor's memory.

Changing the flower arrangement at the gravesite for each season or holiday is a choice many make. Some write a poem or short eulogy about the loved one and have it printed in in their local newspaper.

Ways to remember are so many and varied that a list could be extremely extensive. The primary concern is that you choose what is best for you. Do not be pressured into a plan that will not bring comfort to you.

And remember, you will be progressing in the healing process as time goes by, so expect the manner in which you observe these events to change also.

The joy of the Lord is not there to remove the
pain; it is there to help you bear the pain.

—Unknown

CHAPTER THIRTEEN

Positive Results Of Suicide

This seems like such an awful title to a chapter in this book. And I fully realize as I write these words that they may seem cruel, hurtful, and almost blasphemous. But please remember that I, too, am a survivor of suicide and I hurt just as you do. It just does not seem possible that there could be positive elements or even benefits resulting from the death of a loved one.

But please consider these:

THE SUFFERING IS OVER FOR THE LOVED ONE.

Assuming that your loved one suffered from extreme depression, schizophrenia, bipolar disorder or other heartbreaking mental illness, their time of suffering has ended. As so often occurs, along with the disorder, abuse of alcohol, drugs, or other negative element becomes a part of their life making it even more difficult for them and their family. They try to adapt and cope with life but ultimately cannot go on. The pain is too great and we can only imagine the difficulty and sadness of such a life.

Yes, your heartache has begun, but their life of suffering is over.

YOU LEARN HOW VALUABLE AND PRECIOUS
ARE YOUR FAMILY AND FRIENDS

At no time in your life have you needed others to help and support you as now. And they did. Some people who you never realized loved you so much suddenly appeared to you as they never did before. Now they, too, will always be special to you. "A friend in need is a friend indeed" suddenly becomes a truism to you.

And those in your immediate family seem so much more precious now, too. You want to spend more time with them and express your love for them more earnestly than before.

YOU NOW HAVE A LIFETIME
OPPORTUNITY TO HELP OTHERS

You are now in a very unique group of people who would not have chosen to be in the group at all. Now you have a choice: use the tragedy to center all your thoughts and actions about yourself or use the tragedy to help others. You know your emotional roller coaster and pain very well, so you already know what others are experiencing and you can help them. It may be one-on-one or in a support group but you may be the very person who changes someone else's life for good.

YOU ARE MORE AWARE OF OTHERS
WHO ARE HURTING

This new awareness is not only for other suicide survivors but for any others who you believe are greatly suffering in any way. In psychological studies, there is a state of mind called lateral cognizance. This simply means if you are experiencing a certain positive or negative feeling, you are more aware of others around you who you feel are in the same condition or for example, if you purchase a red automobile, you automatically seem to suddenly notice other red automobiles of the same type. Clothes fall into this category also. If you purchase a certain dress or coat, for example, then you immediately become aware of others who wear the same article of clothing.

With being a suicide survivor, you are keenly aware of not just other survivors, but other hurting people who you now recognize as going through some or much of the same levels of pain you now are experiencing. Under normal circumstances, their plight would not have affected you as much as it now does. You are now more tender to the needs of others.

FOR MANY THIS IS THE BEGINNING OF A MORE PERSONAL RELATIONSHIP TO GOD

More than likely at no time in your life have you been so vulnerable and open to seeking and accepting help. You are confused, possibly angry, sad, depressed, and just want it all to go away. But you know it won't so you realize that you need help in traveling this path of grief.

There are those who get angry with God during this time and vehemently question why he did not interfere and stop the suicide. They rarely think to thank him for all the blessings and material possessions they enjoy, but when such a tragedy occurs, they are quick to condemn him. This is not the norm, but it does happen.

Others do just the opposite and turn to God for help and comfort at this time.

Many survivors have heard the Bible verse found in chapter 3 of the prophetic book of Isaiah. Verse 3 is in the middle of several verses which are foretelling the coming of the Messiah (Jesus Christ). The first part of that verse says: "He is despised and rejected of men; a man of sorrows and acquainted with grief…"

Because he is acquainted (familiar) with grief, he can relate to us and will help us in our time of grief. Daily prayer now is a vital part of one's life as are other avenues of new fellowship with God.

Please consider my motive in discussing these "benefits." I most certainly do not wish to anger you or bring about any additional grief to you. Like you, I would have preferred to incorporate them into my life by almost any other way than through the tragedy of suicide. But it happened, and we have to face it and move forward.

And these can only be positive elements if we determine to accept or pursue them.

If it were not for the darkness of nighttime, we could not see the beauty of the moon and stars. The darker the night, the more majestic the sight.

May we use this "dark time" in our lives to make it a more beautiful place.

A broken heart is fertile ground to the Lord. Until the ground is softened no planting can take place.

—Unknown

CHAPTER FOURTEEN

Depression

Since severe depression or similar mental illness is the leading cause of suicide, with over 90 percent of suicides occurring because of this illness, let us examine it more thoroughly so we might understand the thought process of our departed loved one.

People who die by suicide are not weak people. Most people who take this route are strong people who have a severe, often untreated and greatly misunderstood illness. This is so prevalent in our society with more of our citizens dying by suicide than by homicide.

People die by suicide because they are in intense pain and they want the pain to stop.

So often the people who suffer from depression or a similar illness of the mind do whatever they can to hide the fact of their illness. They are keenly aware of the social stigma associated with mental illness and do all they can to keep others unaware of their illness. Many family survivors of suicides tell heart rendering stories of being totally unaware of the serious problem their loved one had. They should not feel guilty because of this since people with this illness become masters of manipulation and in the hiding of truth and reality. They are victims of the disease just as you are.

SUICIDE: HOW TO COPE WHEN SOMEONE YOU LOVE
HAS TAKEN THEIR OWN LIFE

With young people between the ages of fifteen to twenty-four, suicide is the third leading cause of death. Of the more than 750,000 people who attempt suicide per year, about 41,000 succeed in the attempt. Most of these suicides are due to a depression-related condition.

Many hide their illness or try to "work it out" by themselves. Realistically speaking, this could be compared to someone trying to "work out" cancer or heart problems without any outside evaluations, treatment or professional help.

Depression is a con-artist. It makes the depressed person feel horrible at times and then there are parts of days when things seem to go all right. Day-by-day, the depressed person tries to have some sense of emotional balance while in most cases they know they have a severe problem. Their relationships with family is also a balancing act of trying to "act normal" when they are with family and yet showing a different side of their personality when with friends who have similar problems.

They are often in a state of confusion and hopelessness and yet they do not want to admit it. Often they are prescribed antidepressants but do not want to take them. They feel it will hinder their creativity or thinking ability. Sometimes, they take the medication for a period of time, then, because they believe they can live adequately without the medication, quit taking it. This almost always gives very negative results.

Bipolar disorder, schizophrenia, and depression have been called the "genius diseases." Why? Because many of those who have these illnesses are very intelligent and creative individuals. The creativity of music, art, literature, and other endeavors of this nature provide a temporary avenue of happiness but rarely provides for a lifetime solution. We observe quite often the actor, artist, author or musician who, after a lifetime of success in their field of endeavor, takes their own life.

One very successful and well-known actor who suffers from depression recently stated on a nationally broadcast television program that his depression is "like having a nightmare that never ends." He said that only by faithfully taking the medicine prescribed to him is he able to function. He shared that when in the past he did not take his prescribed medication as he should that he became aggressive and suicidal. The medication, he stated, treats the chemical imbalance in his brain and without the medicine, he simply cannot think rationally.

He was commended for his courage and honesty and he certainly deserved the plaudits.

While untreated depression is the number one cause for suicide, there are, of course, other reasons.

Some people are genetically predisposed to depression. This does not mean they will take their own life, but they are more predisposed to having a severe mental disorder which might possibly lead to suicide. These individuals need to seek professional help to get a valid evaluation and, if necessary, treatment.

There are people who die by suicide because of negative life experiences which they feel are beyond their control or with which they are unable to adequately cope:

Some of these negative life experiences are:

A painful physical problem
A terminal illness
Loss of a job
Loss of a house
Loss of money or other valuable asset
A debilitating accident
Divorce or separation
Death of someone they love

Losing the custody of a child

Military service resulting in mental trauma

Physical pain they feel is beyond their endurance

Loss of purpose or a sense of hopelessness

Physical, sexual or extreme verbal abuse

Pain caused to a loved one through rape, murder, mental cruelty, etc.

Pain caused to themselves through domestic violence, assault, rape, mental or physical abuse

Rejection, especially from family and friends

Rejection by society of people who are somehow different from the norm sexually, mentally, or physically, even economically

Unresolved past problems such as abuse of any sort

Being bullied (this is a problem with adults as well as children)

A feeling of inadequacy that they have not achieved what they or others expect of them

Low self-esteem

Constantly feeling like a failure and unable to deal with it

Drug, alcohol, or other similar abuse

Feeling as if they are trapped in a situation or environment well beyond their ability to be freed from it

Feeling helpless and unable to deal with what they feel is a life of dissatisfaction

Experiencing a great disappointment that was devastating to them

Being humiliated in front of their family or peers

Feeling they are being taken advantage of and cannot rectify the situation

Serious legal problems such as facing possible jail time, a large fine and the accompanying shame that goes along with criminal charges

Feeling very helpless and that things just won't be getting better

Any or several of these aforementioned situations may trigger severe depression. If left untreated and without professional assistance, any of them may lead to suicide, particularly if the person involved is already prone to depression.

Again it cannot be emphasized too strongly that any untreated mental illness including bipolar disorder, schizophrenia, depression, or other such illness may lead to suicide.

The most important thing in communication
is to hear what isn't being said.

—Peter Drucker

CHAPTER FIFTEEN

Treating Depression

I fully realize that the opportunity to help our loved one is past. We can no longer "do all we can" as we once did. However, we may help someone else by being aware of and sharing the avenues of help that are available. This would be a constructive use of the knowledge and experience you now possess.

One of the best ways to prevent suicide is by understanding and treating the mental disorder that causes over 90 percent of all suicides.

There are treatments that can help the person contemplating suicide if they are aware of that which is available and are willing to seek help.

Those concerned individuals, whether the family or the ill person himself, MUST seek professional help and guidance. It will serve no purpose (and I am not qualified) to discuss particular medications such as clozapine which is used in providing possible lessening of risk in schizophrenia, or of antidepressants, atypical anti-psychotic and possibly lithium which may or may not help with those suffering from mood disorders. Only trained and qualified medical professionals can adequately describe, prescribe, and monitor the use of these.

There are currently about twenty-two different medications available and approved by the FDA to treat depression. There is no test to match the correct medication with a patient. The doctor has to make this evaluation in conjunction with the results of the medication and may change the medication several times as the treatment continues.

There is behavior therapy available as well as other means of psychotherapy which might be helpful as short-term therapies.

The key point is that there is help available and most of it centers around either medications or psychotherapy.

If the depression is not too severe, the doctor may begin by "just talking" (psychotherapy) alone and then may add medication at a later date if needed. The doctor is trained to know what questions to ask, how to evaluate the answers and what improvement or lack of improvement they see from this method of treatment. These sessions usually are conducted one to two times per week over a twelve-to-sixteen-week period. Of course this varies depending on the severity of the case and the rate of results.

Those family members assisting the depressed individual should make the doctor aware of any other types of drugs or medication, prescribed or not, that the depressed person is taking. This would also include making the doctor aware of any recent dietary changes, vitamins, or alcohol use.

Patience is needed when waiting for any medication to take effect. Sometimes an almost immediate change is noticed, but often it takes from four-to-twelve weeks to achieve maximum benefit. There may be periods of anxiety, restlessness, agitation, even anger as the medication is consumed. If any of these appear, the doctor should be contacted immediately. This is particularly important at first as the doctor may need to add to the medication, decrease it, or even change to another medicine.

This change in moods, agitation, etc. should not be looked upon as a discouraging factor but one which allows the doctor to be more aware of the result of prescribing the various medicines. They need to be monitored carefully especially during the first few weeks of any medicine usage.

If there is no visible improvement after twelve weeks, the doctor will typically add a second antidepressant, add an additional drug, switch entirely or partially to a different medication or add psychotherapy if that is not already a part of the treatment.

The doctor may ask the patient to participate in a depression rating scale to help determine whether there is improvement or not.

How long the treatments continue is determined by the progress that occurs. In most cases, it should be continued at least nine to twelve months.

There are other forms of treatment and any should be sought only under the guidance and care of professional medical personnel.

Do not feel guilty if you are now more aware of possible avenues you might have pursued to help your loved one. Use what you now know to help others. Make your life's experiences work for you and others, not against you.

Destiny is not a matter of chance;
it is a matter of choice.

—William Jennings Bryan

CHAPTER SIXTEEN

Is Suicide A Selfish Act?

One of the cruelest, most ignorant and hurting comments one might hear about someone who committed suicide is that when they took their own life "they committed the most selfish act anyone could commit."

This comment is wrong, hurtful, and disrespectful. Period.

Sometimes, the person making the comment has a totally different purpose and meaning in saying it. What they really want to portray is the extreme pain the tragedy leaves behind, a pain that supersedes any other. In other words, what they are really saying is, "Suicide is the most painful thing anyone could do to their family and other people who love them."

As I mentioned in another place in this book, the statement that suicide is selfish was said to me soon after my son took his life. Thankfully, I was able to control my anger but I was unable to control my negative thoughts toward this individual until I came to the realization that he was not being unkind. He is a good man and a friend. He simply used the wrong words.

Most suicide deaths are not committed by selfish people, but by hurting people. They are hurt by the mental illness from which they are suffering and the additional problems encountered as a result of the illness. Often, there is accompanying substance abuse, confusion, hopelessness, deep emotional pain, and a constant feeling of despair. It is an act of extreme desperation and pain and they want the pain to stop.

It is typical of any of us to want pain to stop. It is not selfish at all. It is a very human response to physical or mental pain. And the mental judgment of the suicidal person is greatly affected by the illness; they cannot think correctly or consider the many ramifications of their death. They are very ill. They are in great pain and just want it to end. It has absolutely nothing to do with being selfish.

You know your loved one and how much they loved you. They would not have purposely brought this pain to you if they had not been ill.

Try to be patient with those who may use this terrible phrase. They probably mean well.

The remarkable thing about fearing God is that
when you fear God you fear nothing else, whereas
if you do not fear God you fear everything else.

—Oswald Chambers

CHAPTER SEVENTEEN

What Is The Difference Between Depression And Bipolar Disorder?

While there are many variations within both of these mental illnesses, the general characteristics of each are these:

DEPRESSION

General facts:

Like bipolar disorder, depression is a mood disorder.

It is a very complex illness and no one knows exactly what causes it to occur.

It is evident in people of all ages from the very young to the very old.

The best research indicates that depression causes chemical changes in the brain. There are those who claim just the opposite; that depression is caused by chemical changes in the brain. Both may be true.

There may or may not be genetic factors involved.

Some people experience depression for no obvious reason.

Others experience depression when a catastrophic event happens to them.

In addition to other causes, events bringing on depression can include major life changes, a painful or life threatening physical condition, or a stressful environment in which the depress-prone individual cannot control or cope with the negative situation.

Certain medications, the use of alcohol and drug use can also add to the possibility of depression.

COMMON SIGNS OF DEPRESSION

There are many; here are just a few of the more evident signs:

Very anxious about many things. They simply cannot relax. Life is a stressful struggle.

They worry extensively about activities in their lives, deadlines that must be met, work they need to complete, etc.

They feel nervous and do not know the reason for it.

They often have difficulty sleeping. This leads to problems in concentration as well as physical exhaustion. But they try to "keep going" due to their anxiety and need to complete all the tasks required of them.

Increased or decreased appetites can be symptoms of depression.

One common symptom is a continual negative feeling toward life. They are "down" quite often even though there is no apparent reason for the feeling.

Those involved with the person exhibiting any of these negative conditions should immediately assist them in getting the help they need. This is especially true if the person makes statements such as "I would be better off dead" or "I wish I could just end it all." Take these comments seriously.

Just as with any illness, sometimes, the ill person is totally unaware of their condition and needs someone else to help them seek the care they need.

BIPOLAR DISORDER

While depression and bipolar disorder (which is also termed as manic-depressive disorder) are both mood disorders, there are distinctive differences.

People suffering from severe depression are consistently "down" whereas those with a bipolar disorder find themselves alternating between "highs" and "lows." They have drastic mood swings.

When they are "low," it is typically a very negative state of being while the opposite, the "high," often finds the sufferer in a state of euphoria: everything seems to be going great for the individual yet at the same time they may have a feeling of being frantic. They may laugh or talk in an unrealistic manner and not be aware that they are bringing undo attention to themselves.

Another symptom of bipolar disorder is an acute feeling of irritation and often they just want to be left alone.
"Little things" become big problems when they are in this condition.

Others develop an attitude of grandiosity wherein they feel they are being very impressive and dignified. They feel supremely intelligent and important. In this state they often pontificate about the things wrong with society or certain people and give what they believe are all the correct solutions to whatever problem or situation is under consideration at the time. Do not get irritated at them; this is part of the illness and usually occurs when they are in the manic ("high") phase of bipolar disorder.

Agitation is common.

They get sidetracked very easily and are quickly distracted.

They often get very little sleep and yet continue to function. Some get very tired while others seem to have a boundless source of energy regardless of the little amount of sleep they enjoy.

Family and friends quite often get irritated with those with bipolar disorder because they sometimes become very talkative and just do not want to quit talking. Other times, they do not want to talk or even be around others at all.

They are very often impulsive, doing somewhat unusual things in a frenzied and unplanned manner.

Whereas most people act in moderation, the bipolar disorder causes the sufferer to exhibit excessive behavior; they go "overboard" in their behavior at times. It must be remembered that they are not rude, weird, or obnoxious; they are ill.

Those with bipolar disorder are generally very intelligent and are capable of performing a variety of tasks well but find it difficult to maintain permanent employment. It is not because they are lazy or uncommitted; it is because the illness is such that having the ability to have consistent mental and emotional stability is simply beyond their control. One day, they are adept at performing the task and may even enjoy the job whereas the next day finds them wanting to be alone while another day finds them feeling smarter than those in authority and dissatisfied with their working situation. They may feel they are being treated unfairly and do not want to be in that environment any more. They quit, or are fired.

These manic mood swings are a very prevalent and difficult to deal with, many times resulting in drastically interfering with employment, school, family relationships, and social interactions.

With medication and therapy, there is hope; but untreated bipolar disorder leads to a greater risk for suicide.

Proper evaluation and treatment from a professional mental health expert, usually a psychiatrist, is a definite necessity.

It isn't what you have, but what you
are, that makes life worth living.

—Unknown

CHAPTER EIGHTEEN

Clergymen: Compassionate Counselors Or Misguided Ministers?

While I have the highest regard for most of those who call themselves ministers or clergy (whatever title they may have), there are some who express true ignorance, unkindness, and a lack of knowledge of the Bible.

And this glaring dysfunction is most evident when a suicide has been committed.

The survivors need help and the unqualified minister responds in a manner that brings unnecessary grief and dreadful questions as to the eternal fate of the departed loved one.

The minister should be bringing comfort but they are only adding sorrow. The family is already in a state of grief and shock, and do not need more heartache added to their difficult situation.

Please keep in mind that this is rare. Most clergy are extremely capable, willing and ready to offer positive assistance all through the time before, during, and after the funeral and related times of need.

SUICIDE: HOW TO COPE WHEN SOMEONE YOU LOVE
HAS TAKEN THEIR OWN LIFE

From the first notification of my son's suicide and even up to this present day, my pastoral counselors have been more than counselors, they are my friends. I am certain their love and encouragement are greater and more helpful than they will ever realize.

And this is true, I am sure, for others in similar instances.

However, there are those who call themselves ministers who adamantly pontificate their ignorance in making erroneous and hurtful statements during this time of grief.

For instance, one minister told the mother of a twelve-year-old child that her daughter had "gone to hell" because she died by suicide. How horrible, how cruel, and how incorrect!

When I was told this, I had an immediate mixture of sadness and anger. Sadness for the mother and anger at the minister.

This minister is not a minister of God.

Any serious study of the Bible would show this error.

I will mention only one: Samson (who as you probably know was a Christian known for his mighty physical strength).

Samson took his own life after praying to God for strength to push down the pillars of the building where his enemy held him captive. God answered Samson's prayer and he died along with many of his enemies. We find this account in the book of Judges, Chapter 16, verses 23–30.

Would God have given Samson the strength to take his own life and then condemn him to hell? Of course not.

My heart aches for that dear mother and I sincerely hope someone had the opportunity to share the truth with her.

Another minister made definite claims that suicide is an "unforgivable sin" and that any person who takes their own life is ineligible for heaven because God will not forgive the "sin of suicide." If there is anything that should be called unforgivable about this statement, it is that the person who teaches such error calls themselves a minister. Suicide is a mental illness not a moral condition.

There have been church leaders who would not allow a funeral to be conducted in their facility if the person who died did so by way of suicide. This is rare but does happen.

These so-called ministers fit into the category of the arrogant group called the Sadducees as described in the Bible in the book of Matthew, chapter 22, verse 29.

Jesus Himself rebuked this group by saying to them, "Ye do err, not knowing the scriptures, nor the power of God."

The Sadducees were religious leaders who sincerely believed they had superior knowledge of scriptural interpretation when in reality, they were teaching erroneous doctrine. And like most ignorant leaders, they became angry when their error was revealed.

A true minister plays a vital role in the healing process by their kind words and spiritual guidance. Most are so unselfish and reach out in many ways to help those who are suffering.

Ministers are "only human" like you and me, yet they very often sacrifice for others even while they, too, are having times of great personal need.

How does a minister help?

1. By praying with you and for you.

    Prayer is asking for God's help, seeking his will, and, by faith, believing that your prayer will be answered.

    It is talking to the all-powerful and all-loving God of the universe and asking for his help and guidance. Ministers can assist you in praying for you and praying with you.

2. Ministers help by counseling you at a time when you are most confused and vulnerable. They offer sound advice and encouragement at a time when you need it the most.

3. They share positive scriptures that can give you much comfort and peace. If they are true ministers, they do not

simply say what they believe is relevant but they know what the Bible says and where to find comfort and guidance from scripture.

4. Ministers very often follow up on survivors, especially members of their church. This is good and needed because, as you well know, healing is a process and there are distinctive needs at different times in the healing phases.

Do not be hesitant to reach out to your own minster or one to whom you may be referred. You may need to talk with someone and a minister can be a very good friend.

Above all else, regarding the moral aspect of suicide, be firm in your belief that suicide is not due to a lack of love for God, disrespect for family, or other selfish desire. Suicide is a result of the illness of depression or other horribly tormenting mental condition. Those who are mentally ill do not think clearly and very often do not want to die but believe that is the only way to stop their pain.

God is no respecter of persons. He loves everybody. As we read in the scriptures, God did not condemn the sick, he healed them

If you have been blessed with a good and helpful minister, please take time and opportunity to express your appreciation to them with a note, possibly a gift or meal, or at least with words of thankfulness. It is so easy to forget that they, too, need encouragement and words of appreciation.

The Bible was not given to increase our knowledge, but to change our lives.

—D. L. Moody

CHAPTER NINETEEN

Did King David Go To Hell?

What a title for one of the chapters in this book! Why even bother to attempt to prove something most people do not know anything about nor have any interest in knowing about?

The reason I want to include this subject is because it is very relevant to the suicide of your loved one and mine.

First, let us discuss the account of David as found in the Bible in II Samuel, Chapters 11 and 12. Perhaps you might take time to read it for yourself.

Here, we find King David, the writer of most of the Psalms and the very person who slew the giant Goliath earlier in his life.

He who was called, "a man after God's own heart" is, in this passage of scripture, neglecting his duty by staying at home in Jerusalem when he should have been leading his army in battle.

While he remained there, he had occasion to walk on the roof of his house which was a common practice in that day since the roofs were flat by design and provided a cooler place to relax, especially in the cool of the evening.

He saw on a nearby rooftop a very beautiful woman in the process of washing herself. David inquired as to who she was and was told that she was Bathsheba, the wife of Uriah, one of David's most faithful soldiers.

David lusted after her beauty, sent for her, committed adultery with her, and then sent her back to her own house.

Bathsheba conceived and told David that she was "with child."

What was David's response? He sent the general of his army, Joab, to send for Uriah, have him leave the battlefield, return to Jerusalem, and, on the deceitful pretense of wanting to get information from Uriah, asked him how the battle was progressing. His true motive was to get Uriah to spend the night with Bathsheba so that he might "lie with his wife" and be credited with being the father of the coming baby.

David sent a good portion of food to Uriah's house and encouraged him to spend the night there. But Uriah was a man of character and loyalty and did not go to his wife and the comfort of a night's rest at home. He slept instead at the door of the king's house with the servants of the king.

His reason for doing this was that his fellow soldiers and leaders were sleeping in the open fields where the battle was being conducted and he did not want to enjoy pleasure of home, wife, or food while others did not have a similar privilege.

The next day, David tried again to get Uriah to spend the night with Bathsheba. He had Uriah eat and drink with him and had Uriah drink so much intoxicating beverage that he became drunk. David thought this would lower Uriah's resistance against spending the night at home. But he was wrong. Uriah again spent the night with the king's servants.

What was David to do now? He wanted to have people believe that Uriah was the father of the baby to come, not him. This godly man devised a wicked plan. He had Uriah carry a letter to General Joab telling the general to make Uriah be placed in the very front of the hottest battle and then leave him there to be killed. This Joab did and thus Uriah died.

When Bathsheba heard of her husband's death, she mourned for him. Later, David took her for his own wife. A prophet named Nathan was sent from God to rebuke David for all the evil he had done and David truly repented, asking God's forgiveness and mercy.

God did forgive David but the baby died and David experienced much grief and sorrow because of his great sins. He had committed murder, adultery, and was deceitful and selfish.

How does this relate to the matter of suicide? Very simply, this: if someone had known what King David was doing in plotting Uriah's death and putting into effect all the other related horrible acts of sin and violence, they might possibly have made a statement such as, "He surely cannot be a Christian and be doing all these horrible things."

And had David died before he repented of these acts, some may have said, "There's no way he was a Christian. You can't live like that and be a Christian." But they would have been wrong.
David was a Christian.

There is a wonderful statement you may have heard or read which states: "Christians are not perfect, just forgiven."

And God says that whoever comes to him for salvation, he will in no way cast them out from Him. This is difficult for many to believe and I understand their difficulty.

To me, the best illustration of this eternal relationship is this: A person is the mother or father of a child; the child becomes a teenager or older and turns against all the parents taught them as being right and good. The parent is grieved and often angry.
The child even curses their parent, rebukes their parent, mocks their parent, steals from them, and lives a life totally devoid of any love and respect for them.

How bad does the child have to get *not* to be the child of the parents?

There is nothing the child can do to destroy the relationship of parent and child. The fellowship can be broken but not the relationship.

Once the birth takes place, the relationship will never change, regardless of circumstances, good or bad.

Just as in the narrative of the prodigal son, where the selfish young man left home and spent all his money on a wicked lifestyle, yet his father welcomed him when the son "came to himself," repenting of his sins and returned home. Had the young man died while living the wicked lifestyle, he still would have been his father's son.

Accordingly, with many deaths by suicide, at the time of death the person taking their life may have been living a life which could be termed as "a life of sin," possibly a life of rebellion and selfishness. They may have been involved with adultery, drunkenness, or other acts considered immoral and unacceptable.

Their parents had tried with great effort to train them to live a decent life and yet found themselves disappointed and saddened by the way their child was living just prior to their death.

This does not mean that God will reject them. If their relationship with God was one wherein the loved one at some point in their life had accepted the plan of salvation offered by God, then God had become their "Father" and the relationship has never changed.

God's ways are not our ways. We try to think things through from a very limited and biased point of view. God is love and His mercy is beyond our limited capacity to accept.

A human parent may "disown" a child but they can never *not* be the true parent. God never "disowns" his children, no matter how disobedient they may become. He may discipline them or punish them, but he will never "disown" them.

As with the account of David, we cannot be certain of anyone else's relationship to God.

David purposefully acted upon his lust and selfishness whereas a victim of suicide is involved in acts of inordinate behavior and consumption of illicit or prescription drugs and/or alcohol, not for the reason of pleasure or fun, but to ease the pain of depression.

I am convinced that many of the unfortunate people who are arrested for drunken driving or resisting arrest, etc. are more under the influence of a mental disorder than under the influence of a particular stimulant. This is not to excuse those who are not afflicted with this illness and who purposefully and foolishly are aware of the wrong they are doing and do it without regard for others.

What I am stating is that our mental health and law enforcement personnel are usually concerned only with the crime, not the reason the crime was committed.

It is nearly impossible for anyone dealing with a person under the influence of alcohol, drugs, or other mind-altering influence to determine whether the person has become that way because they were foolish or because the pain of living was so terrible they needed to escape it.

There have been many depressed individuals who have immersed themselves in alcohol or drugs who have acted in a way not acceptable or right and have been incarcerated because of it, never receiving the real help they need. The symptom was acted upon but the cause was not addressed.

This is not to state that health officials are not competent nor to say that law enforcement officers do not care.

Most in the mental health field are tremendous workers who genuinely care and are very competent. And most law enforcement officers are very proficient in their jobs and do care for those with whom they come into contact.

I have the greatest respect for both groups of professionals.

It is just that our nation's ability to help those who suffer from mental illnesses is so lacking.

Parents feel so helpless many times because they know their child (or other loved one) needs help but it seems like they just go from one effort to another without ever finding a solution that works.

The victim of suicide should never be judged regarding their lifestyle or spiritual condition. It is not possible for anyone to know for certain another person's relationship to God.

There is the very familiar account of the thief on the cross at the time of the crucifixion of Christ. He was guilty of being a thief and was dying a thief.

But he asked Jesus to "remember me when thou comest into thy kingdom" which was, in essence, saying that he knew he was unworthy of being remembered and accepted into heaven, but he asked Christ for mercy in spite of the life he had lived right up to that time. Did Jesus rebuke him and cast his request aside? No He did not.

Jesus said; "This day thou shalt be with me in paradise."

At the last moment, one who had been a thief and all that goes along with the life of a thief turned to Jesus for salvation and was granted it.

We can never know what has been the discourse between any person and the Savior. Therefore, we should never be so foolish to judge whether or not a person was "right with God" when they died.

However, we can be certain that if sometime during their life, a person had accepted Christ as their personal savior, that they will go to heaven when they die. In the Book of John, we read that if anyone comes to Christ for salvation, there is no way he will cast them out, even if they fall into a life of sin. Remember King David? After his repentance, he prayed for the Lord to restore "the joy of thy salvation," not that he would be "saved all over again."

I fully understand that many who read these words come from many different religious backgrounds and that this may be foreign to them. I am not a theologian, but I have made it a point to completely read through the Bible several times and I do try to study it daily. I have spent a great deal of time in research and study of the topics mentioned and am convinced that man has his theories but God has his truth and that truth is found in the pages of the Bible, not the works or thoughts of man.

We all have our personal beliefs but our beliefs, even those we have accepted as true for many years, can be wrong.

The Bible is absolute and irrefutable.

We can believe it fully and in every situation.

But so many people do not study the Bible and yet feel they know what God will do in various situations.

To know the truth one must know the Bible and the God of the Bible. And no one knows it all but we can know much if we are willing to study.

When the baby of King David and Bathsheba died after living only seven days, David sorrowfully and yet joyfully said, "I shall go to him, but he shall not return to me."

We find two wonderful points here: One, babies who die go to heaven.

Two: David knew he, too, would be going to heaven when he died.

God loves people so much more than our finite minds can absorb and he has made every effort for them to be with him in heaven.

We should not judge a person's relationship with God.

We see outward appearances but only God knows the heart.

"God is our refuge and strength, a
very present help in trouble."

—Psalm 36:7

CHAPTER TWENTY

Is Suicide The Unpardonable Sin?

The short answer is *no*, absolutely not.

People make the erroneous statement that suicide is the unpardonable sin because they are ignorant of what the Bible teaches. As one has said of these people, "They are quick to judge and slow to pray."

God is not surprised when a person takes their life. He is all-knowing, so he knew when the person was born that suicide would be the cause of their death.

It is wrong and contrary to God's will, but suicide does not change the destiny of a person.

When a person accepts Christ as their savior, their eternal destiny is sealed.

In Exodus, we read that the children of Israel put the blood of an animal on the doorpost and lentil of their doorway as they were preparing to leave 430 years of bondage in Egypt.

This assured them that the death angel which would be taking the life of every firstborn of the Egyptians would "pass over" them.

This is the purpose for one of Israel's most important feasts, the Passover Feast, commemorating the leaving of Egypt to journey toward the Promised Land, Israel.

The blood was applied at that time, and all through the Old Testament we read of the sacrificial blood of bulls and goats being offered for the sins of the people.

These many offerings were symbolic of what Jesus would do when he came to this earth.

He became the ultimate and final sacrifice for all our sins when he died, was buried and came back to life, as we celebrate at Easter time.

He voluntarily shed his blood as the payment for our sins and, like the Jews leaving Egypt, we have the assurance that we will not face death.

The Jews were spared physical death because of the blood of animals and we are spared spiritual death because of the blood of Jesus Christ.

It is no longer the blood of bulls and goats, but the precious blood of Jesus that cleanses us from all unrighteousness.

When a person accepts Christ as their Savior, all sin is "under the blood" of Christ.

Regarding our sins, the Bible says in Hebrews 9:22, "… without the shedding of blood there is no remission (forgiveness)."

When Jesus died for us, all our sins were future and yet he still loved us so much he went through horrible pain and agony for us, knowing all the many times we would commit sinful and selfish acts.

Can anything, even a disobedient lifestyle, make God so angry he will separate himself from us? Romans 8:38 states emphatically, "For I am persuaded, that neither death, nor life, nor angels, nor principalities, nor powers, nor things present, nor things to come, nor height, nor depth, nor any other creature, shall be able to separate us from the love of God, which is in Christ Jesus our Lord." NOTHING! NO THING! No deed, no person, no act.

No, God will never leave us nor forsake us.

Psalms 37:28 tells us that "the Lord forsaketh not His saints." Never.

Hebrews 13:5 "... I will never leave thee nor forsake thee." Never.

The only unforgivable sin is the sin of rejecting Jesus Christ as Savior.

Mark 16:16 says, "He that believeth (believes that Jesus died for their sins and accepts him as their only way to heaven) and is baptized (after salvation, as an open expression of what has transpired) shall be saved. But he that believeth not shall be damned (condemned)."

Contrary to what anyone may believe, going to heaven is not determined by weighing a person's good deeds against their bad deeds (even suicide).

Salvation as described in the Bible is based on belief in Jesus Christ as Lord and Savior. Plus nothing, minus nothing.

Suicide is most definitely not the unpardonable sin and someone who has taken their own life has done contrary to what God would want for them; but suicide will not keep someone from going to heaven.

What is unpardonable is that this false teaching prevails as a fact and is taught by those who never effectively or honestly studied the scriptures. Like the Sadducees in Matthew 22:29, they "err, not knowing the scriptures, nor the power of God."

He giveth power to the faint; and to them that
have no might he increaseth strength."

—Isaiah 40:29

CHAPTER TWENTY-ONE

Peace With God

At the risk of offending those who are of other beliefs than my own, I feel an obligation to relay how I have been able to have a great sense of peace through the devastating death by suicide of my son. It is not because I am any more spiritual or stronger in handling a crisis; it is because of the relationship I am privileged to have with God.

This relationship is available to every person, young or old, rich or poor, intelligent or not so intelligent, and any other person willing to give it sincere consideration.

And please pardon me as I relate my personal spiritual journey. Remember this book is "friend to friend" and I share it with you as I would any of my friends.

As a young child, I was taught that my destiny regarding going to heaven or hell was a mute point until I became twelve years old.

Up to that point, I was told I had not reached the "age of accountability" and that I did not have anything to worry about.

This sounded good to me and I accepted that erroneous teaching until I reached my twelfth birthday; then I wondered what I should do.

I was told that if I was "sincere," all would be well. That sounded good but did not bring any real answers to the questions I had.

I was sincere about a lot of things but had been proved to be sincerely wrong in many of them.

I overheard an aunt saying that to be "right with God" one had to be consecrated. I had no idea what that meant, but it sounded really spiritual and something to be desired. But I did not know how to go about getting "consecrated."

When I was about fifteen years old, I participated in playing on a church softball team wherein we competed against other church teams of various faiths. I would listen to the different ministers as they coached their teams and discovered that ministers could also be somewhat unkind and say things that I felt were not very nice. Most of them were very pleasant men and did a great job in being a good example to the young people participating. But some did just the opposite.

At that time, I had a mental "holy chain of command" regarding the way God looked at everybody. First, most important and special was God; then came ministers, choir members, old people who had been Christians a long time, other church attenders, and then me. For ministers to be so unkind and unChristlike was a shock to my thinking. I now realize they are subject to the same difficulties as we all are and I have a great respect for most of them.

About that time, the thought came to me that some (if not all) of the coach/ministers had to be wrong in what they believe. They taught different doctrines, therefore some had to be incorrect. Maybe they all were wrong. As a typical young fellow, I did not think much about spiritual matters but when I did I had no idea of what was true doctrine and what was not true doctrine.

To be a member of the church softball team, each player had to attend at least one church service per week. So I went to church, one service per week. No one else in my family attended the church and I usually found myself on the back row with other young fellows who were there for the same reason. I did not pay much attention to what was being preached.

As I recall, I had heard of the baby Jesus, Jesus on the cross, Adam and Eve, and, I think, Noah and the ark. That was the full extent of my Bible "knowledge" at that point in my life.

But one Sunday morning, the minister did something I had never seen a grown man do. He cried.

As he was preaching, he was so concerned that some of those who were listening to his message were not prepared for death and what comes after death that he cried as he preached.

This caught my attention and I started listening. As I listened, I realized that what he was saying not only made sense but he based it all on the Bible, not his opinion.

At the end of his sermon, I responded to the "altar call," went to the front of the church and prayed, asking God to let me be a Christian too.

I did what the minister said I needed to do to be ready to go to heaven when I died.

Certainly, I did not understand everything, but I understood enough to do what I was told should be done.

My life was changed. I had real peace and an assurance that my eternal destiny was assured. As with all other Christians, I did not become "perfect," but I knew I was forgiven for all my sins, and I knew I would go to heaven when I died. Not because of my goodness but because of God's mercy and love.

Of course, I cannot remember all that was said that day, but in the many years since that morning, I have grown to understand the wonderful joy of salvation. And that is what I would like to share with you.

It is so profound and yet it is so simple that a child can do it. It only takes our faith and God's mercy.

Here it is:

First, realize that the Bible says, "Ye must be born again" (John 3:7). Not another physical birth, but a spiritual birth. Jesus told a man named Nicodemus, a ruler of the Jews, "Verily, verily, I say unto thee, except a man be born again, he cannot see the kingdom of heaven." (John 3:3). Nicodemus questioned Jesus about how a man could be born again; could he enter the second time into his mother's womb? Jesus answered by telling him that what is born of the flesh is flesh (human birth) and what is born of the Spirit (God's gift of spiritual birth) is spirit.

In other words, a person cannot become a Christian unless they have this new birth, which only comes from God. But how does this new birth happen? What must a person do to be "saved?"

The first thing to do is to realize and admit that you are a sinner. We have all sinned; so from God's point of view, no one is better or worse than anyone else. "For all have sinned and come short of the glory of God." (Romans 3:23)

And because we are sinners, we are condemned to spiritual death (separation from God when we die). "For the wages (payment) of sin is death." (Romans 6:23)

We all have an appointment with death, but that appointment does not have to be feared unless we are unprepared. "… it is appointed unto men once to die, but after this the judgment." (Hebrews 9:27)

But thankfully, God loves us and has a plan for our salvation.

In the Bible, it says, "God so loved the world (the people in the world) that He gave His only begotten son (Jesus), that whosoever believeth in Him should not perish but have everlasting life." (John 3:16)

Jesus tells us why he came to this earth, "… I am come that they might have life and that they might have it more abundantly." (John 10:10)

He went from being the baby in the stable to being the tortured savior on the cross, so we can spend eternity with him in heaven.

Jesus paid for your sins and he suffered and died for you. "… He hath made Him (Jesus, who knew no sin) to be sin for us… that we might be made the righteousness of God in Him." (2 Corinthians 5:21)

In other words, we cannot pay the great price required to pay for our sins, so Jesus paid it for us. He shed his blood on the cross as the payment for our sins. "… without shedding of blood is no remission (forgiveness)."

Just as in the Old Testament, we read of the many animal sacrifices made which required shedding the blood of each animal, so Jesus became the sacrificial offering that once and for all time paid the price for all our sins.

What love to do this for us! In Romans 5:8, we read, "… God commendeth His love toward us, in that, while we were yet sinners, Christ died for us."

We cannot understand all that was involved in what God did for us, but we can easily understand that your degrading sins and my degrading sins were laid upon a holy and pure Jesus and he died in our place. He was our willing substitute.

Can't we just live a good life and go to heaven? No, we can never live a life good enough to go to heaven.

If we could, then why did Jesus have to die to save us from our sins? "God… commandeth all men everywhere to repent." (Acts 17:30)

Repent simply means to change one's mind, to agree with God that we are a sinner and that what Jesus did on the cross provided the only way we get to heaven. Jesus said in John 14:6, "… I am the way (the only way), the truth (the true way), and the life (eternal); no man cometh unto the father but by me."

So what do we do?

In Acts 16: 30, 31, the Philippian jailer asked the Apostle Paul and his coworker Silas, "… Sirs, what must I do to be saved?"

The answer? "And they said, 'Believe on The Lord Jesus Christ and thou shalt be saved…'"

To believe means "to trust, have confidence in, have faith in, accept as true."

To "believe on the Lord Jesus Christ" for salvation means the same; to have faith in the Bible that what God has said is true, that Jesus did die to pay for your sins, to trust him and him alone to take you to heaven when you die, to accept him as your personal savior.

Not by your works but by his sacrifice for you on the Cross of Calvary.

Believe with all your heart that he bore your sins, died in your place, was buried, and was then resurrected to live forevermore, just as you can live forevermore in heaven if you accept him as savior.

It is a choice each of us have to make.

To refuse to do anything is making the choice to refuse him.

"But as many as received Him, to them gave He power to become the sons of God, even to them that believe on His Name." (John 1:12)

Can anyone do this?

Yes, they can if they want to. "For whosoever shall call upon the Name of the Lord shall be saved." (Romans 10:13)

In simple terms, anybody who chooses to pray to God, asking Him to save them by accepting Jesus Christ as their Savior because of what he did on the cross, they *shall* be saved, a definite promise of God, not just a possibility or vain hope.

Every one of us is a "whosoever."

God loves everybody and he gives each of us an equal opportunity to be prepared for heaven.

Whether we like to admit it or not, we are all sinners from birth.

No one had to teach us to lie, to steal, to be deceitful, to be lazy, disobey, etc. We were born with a sin nature and will die with it unless we are "born again." Surely you, like me, realize you have sinned.

And do you, like me, feel bad about the wrong things we have done and want to change to a better life? This "feeling bad" (guilt) about our sins and wanting to change for the better is called repentance.

There is in Luke 18:13, a sweet and heartfelt cry made by some one who realized they needed help. The dear person simply cried out to God, "God be merciful to me, a sinner."

This is what I did that Sunday morning so long ago and this is what I am asking you to do if you are not a Christian but would like to be one.

You might pray this prayer (and please remember it is not the prayer that saves your soul, it is your believing what God has said and by accepting a person, the Lord Jesus Christ, as your Savior):

> *Dear God, I admit I am a sinner.*
> *I believe Jesus died for my sins when He died on the cross.*
> *I believe His shed blood, His death and resurrection were for me, too.*
> *I now receive Jesus as my Savior.*

I know He is the only way to Heaven and I am not trusting anything or anyone but Him for salvation.

Please forgive me of all my sins and take me to Heaven when I die.

Thank you Jesus for forgiving me of all my sins.

Thank you for giving me salvation and everlasting life.

I love you and want to serve you because you love me and have done so much for me.

Amen.

Of course, the words one prays does not have to be exactly as these; the truth of the plan of salvation is what is most important.

You did your part and God did his part. You did the asking and God did the saving. All of it.

Jesus gave his Son and you accepted his gift. A gift does not have to be earned, only accepted.

It is so simple that anyone can understand it and yet it is so profound that an Almighty God devised it.

What should a new Christian do now?

First, thank God for the marvelous work he just did in your life.

Tell others who you think might be happy about your decision.

Then find a church where the Bible is taught, not a "feel-good," liberal church that teaches a social lecture each week, but one where the minister teaches the truths of the Bible.

Start every day with praying to your new best friend and talk with him often during the day.

Read the Bible.

Many new Christians start with the Book of John in the New Testament. Pray for understanding as you read.

You will grow more knowledgeable and at a quicker rate if you attend a church where the Bible is taught consistently in Sunday School and in the regular services.

In closing this chapter, may I again state for those who have different religious backgrounds and who may find this chapter irritating at best, that my motive is simply to share why I have had great peace during the time of grieving over my son. I have found that grief and joy can walk hand-in-hand.

I certainly do not want to be offensive in any way; my motive is to help.

Jesus is called The Prince of Peace, and he has proved to me since that dreadful day of my son's suicide that he gives peace even in the midst of heartache.

If this chapter helps even one person become ready for heaven and receives what the Bible calls, "the peace that passes understanding," it will have been well worth the effort.

"God shall wipe away all tears."

—Revelation 7:17

CHAPTER TWENTY-TWO

Concluding Comments

You have read the book.
With all my heart, I hope it has been a help to you.

May we have a few concluding remarks and reminders?

If you are still in the first year of your tragedy, please remember that this is the hardest year: it will get better.

And even after the first year, there is much more healing needed.

The first year brings so many "firsts," and every year after that still finds sadness and heartache.

It was so difficult to tell that first person and it still hurts to talk about it, especially to certain people.

The first birthday, anniversary, or holiday since the loved one's death was hard and still is.

The first feeling of being "lost," lonely, and very sad never seems to leave for very long.

The first time you heard their name after the death, it really brought pain—and still does.

It is so painful to look at pictures of the loved one.

You cry more often now and so easily.

Do you know what all of this means?

It means you are normal.

You hurt because you love. Love is often accompanied by some element of pain.

You cannot grieve without loving.

Take one day at a time. And each day just take small steps. What can you do today that will help?

Be patient with yourself and others.

Express your emotions freely to those who care. It will help you and them.

Honor your departed loved one, but do not let their memory and your love for them become your primary focus in life. There are others who need you and need your love and help.

Talk with those who will be of help to you, not negative people. You chose those with whom you wish to talk.

Take a walk. Do some exercise, even if it is very minimal. It will release tension.

Cry as long as you want and as often as you want. In this instance, crying is a wonderful expression of your love as well as your grief.

Get out of the house. Go to a store, visit friends. At least get outside for a while. It will be good for you.

Telephone loved ones. It will be good to hear their voice and they want to hear your voice as well.

Turn your anger into forgiveness. Forgive others and forgive yourself. Bitterness and anger are extremely damaging to the person who holds these in their hearts.

Accept the fact that there will always be some loneliness in your life.

This is hard, but you can live with this. Loneliness is the great price we pay for loving someone.

It will probably never go away but we can use it to be more sensitive toward others who are lonely; we know exactly how they feel and we may have opportunity to help them get through their time of sorrow.

Rather than letting the tragedy use you and control you, use the tragedy to help others.

Resolve to make an effort to be aware of the needs of others and to use the suicide in a way that brings helpful and positive results.

You cannot change what has happened but you can let what happened change you for good.

As time goes by, you will remember the days when it seemed as if you just simply could not go on; the pain was so intense that you felt life was not worth living.

What you will discover is that you will always miss your loved one, but instead of the terrible pain inside, It has now been replaced by a gentle ache.

Have courage and faith, dear friend. It will get better.

"Peace is not the absence of trouble;
peace is the presence of God."

—Unknown

BIBLIOGRAPHY

SUICIDE AND MENTAL ILLNESS
An Unquiet Mind: A Memoir of Moods and Madness
Kay Redfield Jamison, PhD
Alfred A. Knopf, 1995

UNDERSTANDING DEPRESSION
What We Know and What You Can Do About It
J. Raymond DePaulo, Jr., M.D.
John Wiley and Sons, Inc., 2002

WHY SUICIDE?
Questions and Answers about Suicide, Suicide Prevention, and
Coping with the Suicide of Someone You Know (2nd Edition)
Eric Marcus
HarperOne, 2010

NIGHT FALLS FAST
Understanding Suicide
Kay Redfield Jamison, Ph.D.
Alfred A. Knopf, 1999

DARKNESS VISIBLE
William Styron
Random House, 1990

DEMYSTIFYING PSYCHIATRY
A Resource for Patients and Families
Charles Zorumski and Eugene Rubin
Oxford University Press, 2010

DYING TO BE FREE
A Healing Guide for Families After a Suicide
Beverly Cobain and Jean Larch
Hazelden Foundation, 2006

AFTER SUICIDE LOSS
Coping With Your Grief
Bob Baugher, PhD, and Jack Jordan, 2002
Available through the American Foundation for
Suicide Prevention, www.afsp.org

HEALING AFTER THE SUICIDE OF A LOVED ONE
Ann Smolin and John Guinan
Simon and Shuster, 1993

AFTER SUICIDE
John H. Hewitt
Westminster, 1980

THE NOONDAY DEMON
An Atlas of Depression
Andrew Solomon
Scribner, 2001

NOVEMBER OF THE SOUL
The Enigma of Suicide
George Howe Colt
Scribner, 2006

A SPECIAL SCAR
The Experience of People Bereaved by Suicide
Allison Wertheimer
Routledge, 2001

TOUCHED BY SUICIDE
Hope and Healing After Loss
Michael F. Myers, M.D., and Carla Fine
Gotham Books, 2006

SURVIVORS OF SUICIDE
Rita Robinson and Phyllis Hart
New Page Books, 2001

SUICIDE OF A CHILD
Adina Wrobleski
Centering Corp., 2002

DEAD RECKONING
A Therapist Confronts His Own Grief
David C. Treadway
BasicBooks, 1996

LAY MY BURDEN DOWN
Unravelling Suicide and The Mental Health Crisis
Among African Americans
Alvin F. Poussaint, M.D., and Amy Alexander
Beacon Press, 200 1

REACHING OUT AFTER SUICIDE
What's Helpful and What's Not
Linda H. Kilburn, M.S.W.
KP Associates, LLC
(KPAMASS@aol.com)

SUICIDE AND ITS AFTERMATH
Understanding and Counseling The Survivors
Edward Dunne, John McIntosh, and Karen Dunne-Maxim, (Eds.)
W.W.Norton and Company, 1987

SILENT GRIEF
Living in the Wake of Suicide
Christopher Lucas and Henry Seiden
Jessica Kingsley Publishers, 2007

SUICIDE SURVIVORS HANDBOOK
Expanded Edition
Trudy Carlson
Benline Press, 2000

NO ONE SAW MY PAIN
Why Teens Kill Themselves
Andrew Slaby and Lili Frank Garfinkle
W.W.Norton and Company, 1995

BEFORE THEIR TIME
Adult Children's Experiences of Parental Suicide
Mary and Maureen Stimming
Temple University Press, 1999

BLUE GENES
A Memoir of Loss and Survival
Christopher Lukas
Doubleday, 2008

THE EMPTY CHAIR
The Journey of Grief After Suicide
Beryl Glover
In Sight Books, 2000

THE SUICIDE INDEX
Putting My Father's Death in Order
Joan Wickersham
Harcourt, Inc., 2008

SANITY AND GRACE
A Journey of Suicide, Survival, and Strength
Judy Collins
Tarcher/Penguin, 2003

REMEMBERING GARRETT
One Family's Battle With a Child's Depression
U.S. Senator Gordon H. Smith
Caroll and Graf, 2006

NEVER REGRET THE PAIN
Loving and Losing a Bipolar Spouse
Scl Erder Yackley
Helm Publishing, 2008

A FORCE UNFAMILIAR TO ME
A Cautionary Tale
Jane Butler
Hamlet Books, 1998

PARTICULARLY HELPFUL FOR CHILDREN AND TEENS

TEENS:

AFTER
Francis Chalifour
Tundra, 2005

AFTER A SUICIDE
Young People Speak Up
Susan Kuklin
Putnam Publishing Group, 1994

YOUNG CHILDREN

AFTER A PARENT'S SUICIDE
Helping Children Heal
Margo Requarth, Healing Hearts Pres, 2006

AFTER A SUICIDE
A Workbook for Grieving Kids
The Dughy Center
www.doughy.org 503-775-5683

BUT I DIDN'T SAY GOODBYE
For Parents and Professionals Helping Child Suicide Survivors
Barbara Rubel
Griefwork Center, Inc., 2000

CHILD SURVIVORS OF SUICIDE
A Guidebook for Those Who Care for Them
Rebecca Parkin and Karen Dunne-Maxim
Available through www.afsp.org, 1995

MY UNCLE KEITH DIED
Carol Ann Loehr
Trafford Publishing, 2006

SOMEONE I LOVE DIED BY SUICIDE
A Story for Child Survivors and Those Who Care for Them
Doreen Cammarata
Grief Guidance, Inc., 2000

MATERIALS PRODUCED ESPECIALLY FOR WOMEN

IN HER WAKE
A Child Psychiatrist Explores the Mystery of Her Mother's Suicide
Nancy Rappaport
Basic Books, 2009

MY SON... MY SON
A Guide to Healing After Death, Loss or Suicide
Iris Bolton and Curtis Mitchell
The Bolton Press, 1995

NO TIME TO SAY GOODBYE
Surviving the Suicide of a Loved One
Carla Fine
Doubleday, 1998

MATERIALS PRODUCED ESPECIALLY FOR MEN

MEN AND GRIEF
A Guide for Men Surviving the Death of a Loved One and a Resource
for Caregivers and Mental Health Professionals
Carol Staudacher
New Harbinger Publications, 1991

REAL MEN DO CRY
A Quarterback's Inspiring Story of Tackling Depression and Surviving
Suicide Loss
Eric Hipple, with Dr. Gloria Horsley and Dr. Heidi Horsley
Quality of Life Publishing Company, 2008

WHEN A MAN FACES GRIEF
A Man You Know is Grieving: 12 Practical Ideas to Help You Heal
From Loss
Thomas Golden and James Miller

Willowgreen Publishing, 1998

WHEN SUICIDE COMES HOME
A Father's Diary and Comments
Paul Cox
Bolton Press, 2002

SWALLOWED BY A SNAKE
The Gift of the Masculine Side of Healing
Thomas R. Golden
Golden Healing Publishing, 1996

ONLINE RESOURCES

www.afsp.org

One of the best. This is the online address for the American Foundation for Suicide Prevention. This organization has a wealth of information regarding all aspects of suicide.

www.suicide.org is a nonprofit organization which is quite helpful and has a wide array of helpful information.

www.groww.org offers online support groups organized by the type of loss and relationship.

www.livingthroughsuicide.invisionzone.com is another online support group.

www.survivorsofsuicide.com is a very good source for general information about surviving suicide loss.

www.suicidegrief.com is a survivor discussion board.

www.siblings.com is an online address created by a survivor after she lost her sister to suicide.

www.pos-ffos.com The address refers to "Parents of Suicides and Friends and Family of Suicides," a support group.

www.suicidereferencelibrary.com has a very good list of available resources.

www.thegiftofkeith.org was created by a family member who survived a suicide and wishes to share helpful information and resources.

www.save.org is a nonprofit organization which has as its primary purpose to educate the public about depression and suicide.

www.swcideinfo.ca is a resource library, offering a variety of materials including pamphlets, information kits and literature.

www.sprc.org has an extensive online library of information and an excellent array of helpful materials.

SURVIVOR OUTREACH PROGRAM

The very reputable and extremely helpful American Foundation for Suicide Prevention offers a wide variety of materials and services.·

Probably one of the most helpful services they offer is their "Survivor Outreach Program."

This program links the recent survivor of suicide with someone who truly understands what the survivor is going through and is willing and very able to help them.

Recently-bereaved survivors are connected with trained volunteers who know what to discuss and how to best help.

Each volunteer has also lost a loved one to suicide so knows exactly the pain and emotional difficulties the newly-bereaved is facing.

AFSP volunteers were moved to help others after they benefited so much by sharing their own experiences. Now they offer the same opportunity for those who choose to take advantage of the resource.

Possibly you "just need to talk" to someone. This would be an excellent place to contact for that and other help.

Contact them at www.afsp.org or by calling 1 888-333-ASFP (2377)

ORGANIZATIONS

The following organizations have proven to be very helpful for suicide survivors:

The American Foundation for Suicide Prevention
120 Wall Street, 29111 Floor
New York, New York
10005 1-888-333-AFSP
www.afsp.org

American Association of Suicidology
202-237-2280
www.suicidology.org

The Compassionate Friends
630-990-0010
www.compassionatefriends. org

American Psychological Association
800-374-2721
www.apa.org

The Dougy Center
The National center for Grieving Children and Families
503-775-5683
www.dougy.org

International Association for Suicide Prevention
www.iasp.info/postvention.php

And the National Suicide Prevention Hotline Lifeline is a suicide prevention service available to anyone who finds themselves in a suicide crisis.

They operate 24/7 and the services are offered at no cost.

They route those calling to the closest suicide prevention center in the area.

And they can provide immediate assistance to anyone seeking mental health services. Those who need help and those who need to help others may call at no cost and all calls are confidential.

The number is 1-800-273- TALK (8255)

COMFORTING SCRIPTURES

Just as we receive strength for our bodies from nourishing food, we can receive strength for our soul—the real you—from the Bible.

Here are just a few wonderful scriptures that I pray will bring comfort and blessings to you:

(I read this first verse every day and have claimed it as my favorite and most helpful verse):

Isaiah 41:10 "Fear thou not, for I am with thee; be not dismayed, for I am thy God. I will strengthen thee, yea, I will help thee; yea, I will uphold thee with the right hand of my righteousness."

Other precious verses:

"But I am poor and needy; yet the Lord thinketh on me; thou art my help and my deliverer; make no tarrying, O my God." — Psalm 40:17

"Trust in the Lord with all thine heart; and lean not unto thine own understanding. In all thy ways acknowledge Him and He shall direct thy paths." —Proverbs 3: 5, 6

"The name of the Lord is a strong tower; the righteous runneth into it, and is safe." —Proverbs 18: 10

"God is our refuge and strength; a very present help in trouble." —Psalm 46: I

"I have set the Lord always before me: because He is at my right hand, I shall not be moved." —Psalm 16:8

"Cast thy burden upon the Lord, and He shall sustain thee: He shall never suffer the righteous to be moved." —Psalm 55:22

"Peace I leave with you, my peace I give unto you; not as the world giveth, give I unto you. Let not your heart be troubled, neither let it be afraid." —John 14:27

"These things have I spoken unto you, that in me ye might have peace. In the world ye shall have tribulation; but be of good cheer; I have overcome the world." —John 16:33

"For God hath not given us the spirit of fear; but of power, and of love, and of a sound mind." —II Timothy 1:7

"Casting all your care upon Him, for He careth for you." —I Peter 5:7

"Thou wilt keep him in perfect peace whose mind is stayed on Thee, because he trusteth in Thee." —Isaiah 26:3

"The Lord is my strength and song, and is become my salvation." —Psalm 118:14

"Thou art my hiding place and my shield; I hope in Thy word." —Psalm 119:114

"In my distress I called upon the Lord, and He heard me." —Psalm 120:1

"… weeping may endure for a night, but joy cometh in the morning." —Psalm 30:5

"The Lord is good. A strong hold in the day of trouble; and He knoweth them that trust in Him." —Nahum 1:7

"For He hath not despised nor abhorred the affliction of the afflicted; neither hath He hid His face from them; but when he cried unto Him, He heard." —Psalm 22:24

"I love the Lord, because He hath heard my voice and my supplications." —Psalm 116:1

"Hast thou not known? Hast thou not heard, that the everlasting God, the Lord, the Creator of the ends of the earth, fainteth not, neither is weary? There is no searching of His understanding.

He giveth power unto the faint; and to them that have no might he increaseth strength; even the youths shall faint and be weary, and the young men shall utterly fall.

But they that wait upon the Lord shall renew their strength; they shall mount up with wings as eagles; they shall run, and not be weary; and they shall walk, and not faint." —Isaiah 40:28–31

"I sought the Lord and He heard me." —Psalm 34: 4

"The Lord is nigh unto them that are of a broken heart..." — Psalm 34:18

"He healeth the broken in heart, and bindeth up their wounds." —Psalm 147:3

"In my distress I called upon the Lord, and cried to my God: and He did hear my voice out of His temple, and my cry did enter into His ears." —II Samuel 22:7

There are many, many more words of encouragement we can receive from God's Word, the Bible. Perhaps reading Psalm 23 would be a particular comfort to you just now.

Verse I says, "The Lord is MY shepherd," so it is very personal and wonderful.

Why not read it and (if you have not already done so) claim Jesus Christ as YOUR "Good Shepherd?"

I BELIEVE

(Written on the wall of a concentration camp in Germany
during World War II)

I believe in the sun even when
it is not shining.

I believe in love even when
I feel it not.

I believe in God even when
He is silent...

Peace to You!

Pilgrim, in thy upward journey,
　　Heavy laden, sore oppressed,
Tune thy heart to Love's sweet message,
　　Jesus giveth peace and rest.

Tribulations oft beset thee,
　　Garments torn and travel-stained;
One has trod this path before thee,
　　And for thee hath vict'ry gained.

He hath borne our grief and sorrow,
　　He hath carried all our woe;
Cast thy burden on the Saviour,
　　Hear Him whisper, sweet and low,—

Hast thou doubted His dear presence
　　In affliction's saddest hour?
Upward look! His smile will greet thee;
　　Know His wonder-working power.

"Peace to you!" His voice bids sorrow cease;
"Peace to you!" How hope and joy increase;
"Peace to you!" Troubled heart, there's always peace,
　　When we hear the voice of Jesus.

　　　　　　　　　—*Mrs. Norman H. Camp*

RESOLVE

I would encourage you to make the following resolution:

"I resolve from this time forward to use the death by suicide of my loved one in such a way that it will benefit others and give me a way to bring victory out of what could have been defeat.

"I will not live in a state of guilt or despair, but will do what I can to use this tragedy and my life to help others who are hurting as they also walk this difficult pathway.

"I will still hurt at times. I will still cry at times. But with God's help, I will use my life and the death of my loved one in a fruitful, positive manner that will give my life purpose and meaning and will be a life that brings comfort to others while being a credit to the memory of my dear loved one."

"I may stumble but I resolve to not quit."

"You will never realize how much you need God until all you have is God."

—Unknown

SUICIDE

How to Cope When Someone You Love Has Taken Their Life

William J. Henry

"If you are mourning the loss of a loved one due to death by suicide, this book will be a help and comfort to you. William J. Henry has walked the same emotional path you are now walking and knows firsthand of that about which he writes."

"The author gently leads the reader from the darkness of despair to a new and hopeful place. It is written as one friend to another and will bring encouragement to all who read it."

"Any pastor or other church leader and any others who have the daunting task of counseling or comforting those who are going through this time of healing will find the book very practical and helpful. It gives great insight into what should be said and what should not be said during this painful time."

"This book fills a void that has existed for many years. We often take pity on the survivors of suicide but we do not know what to say or do. This book not only fills that void but also uniquely equips the survivor themselves regarding what to expect and how to handle the pressures and pain of the healing process.

Get this book into their hands and it will bring comfort to their heart."

ABOUT THE AUTHOR

William J. Henry has been an educator for over forty years both in the public school sector and in Christian Schools, having been a teacher and school administrator. Henry co-authored a WV State History curriculum which has been used in Christian Schools in that state for a number of years. He also served for fourteen years as a field representative for Bob Jones University, Greenville SC.

Henry often gives education-related seminars, workshops, and graduation addresses. Henry and his wife have been married for forty-eight years and have been blessed with four children and nine grandchildren. They make their home in Parkersburg WV where both are active members in their church.

CPSIA information can be obtained
at www.ICGtesting.com
Printed in the USA
LVOW11s1814111116
512630LV00002B/162/P